Children's Issues, Laws and Programs Series

Foster Care and African-American Youth

CHILDREN'S ISSUES, LAWS AND PROGRAMS SERIES

Federal Programs for Troubled Youth
Killian Lucero
2009. ISBN: 978-1-60692-318-4

Federal Programs for Troubled Youth
Killian Lucero
2009. ISBN: 978-1-60876-701-4
(Online book)

Child Sexual Abuse: Pitfalls in the Substantiation Process
Anna Aprile, Cristina Ranzato, Melissa Rosa Rizzotto and Paola Facchin
2009. ISBN: 978-1-60741-427-8

Diet Quality of American Young Children
Calvin G. Parker (Editor)
2009. ISBN: 978-1-60692-771-7

Diet Quality of American School-Age Children
Kelly B. Volkarsky (Editor)
2009. ISBN: 978-1-60692-776-2

National School Lunch Program Assessment
Manuel P. Borges (Editor)
2009. ISBN: 978-1-60692-972-8

Reading First Impact Study
Beth C. Games , Howard S. Bloom, James J. Kemple, Robin Tepper Jacob, Beth Boulay, Laurie Bozzi, Linda Caswell, Megan Horst, W. Carter Smith, Robert G. St.Pierre, Fatih Unlu, Corinne Herlihy and Pei Zhu
2009. ISBN: 978-1-60741-529-9

Vulnerable and Disconnected Youth: Background and Policies
Dierk Neumann (Editor)
2010 ISBN: 978-1-60741-488-9

Foster Care and African-American Youth
Joanna Kaczmarek (Editor)
2010 ISBN: 978-1-60741-541-1

Preschool Children: Physical Activity, Behavioral Assessment and Developmental Challenges
Leone Colombo and Rachele Bianchi
2010 ISBN: 978-1-60876-026-8

Child Development and Child Poverty
Anselm Fiedler and Isidor Kuester
2010 ISBN: 978-1-60741-816-0

Child Protection, the Courts and Social Workers
Terrance R. Langely (Editor)
2010 ISBN: 978-1-60741-279-3

Child Labor in America
Ian C. Rivera and Natasha M. Howard (Editor)
2010 ISBN: 978-1-60876-769-4

Child Abduction Resources
Melanie H. Wilson (Editor)
2010 ISBN: 978-1-61668-247-7

Adam Walsh Child Protection and Safety Act: Analysis and Law
Terrell G. Sandoval (Editor)
2010 ISBN: 978-1-61668-808-0

Adam Walsh Child Protection and Safety Act: Analysis and Law
Terrell G. Sandoval (Editor)
2010 ISBN: 978-1-61668-808-0
(Online book)

Working with the Courts in Child Protection
Raymond T. Devon (Editor)
2010 ISBN: 978-1-61668-303-0

Working with the Courts in Child Protection
Raymond T. Devon (Editor)
2010 ISBN: 978-1-61668-303-0
(Online book)

CHILDREN'S ISSUES, LAWS AND PROGRAMS SERIES

FOSTER CARE AND AFRICAN-AMERICAN YOUTH

JOANNA KACZMAREK
EDITOR

Nova Science Publishers, Inc.
New York

LIBRARY OF CONGRESS CATALOGING-IN-PUBLICATION DATA

Available upon request.
ISBN: 978-1-60741-541-1

Published by Nova Science Publishers, Inc. † New York

CONTENTS

Preface		**ix**
Chapter 1	African American Children in Foster Care: HHS and Congressional Actions Could Help Reduce Proportion in Care *U. S. Government Accountability Office*	**1**
Chapter 2	Foster Care: State Practices for Assessing Health Needs, Facilitating Service Delivery, and Monitoring Children's Care *U. S. Government Accountability Office*	**23**
Chapter 3	Child Welfare: HHS Actions Would Help States Prepare Youth in the Foster Care System for Independent Living *U. S. Government Accountability Office*	**75**
Chapter 4	Hearing on Racial Disproportionality in Foster Care, United States House of Representatives, Subcommittee on Income Security and Family Support *Child Welfare League of America*	**103**
Chapter 5	Statement of Daryle Conquering Bear, Former Foster Youth, Colorado before the Subcommittee on Income Security and Family Support of the House Committee on Ways and Means: Hearing on Racial Disproportionality in Foster Care	**115**

Chapter 6	Testimony of Casey Family Programs, Hearing on Racial Disproportionality in Foster Care, before the Subcommittee on Income Security and Family Support, U.S. House of Representatives *Oronde Miller*	**119**
Chapter 7	Trends in Foster Care and Adoption—FY 2002-FY 2007 *Joanna Kaczmarek*	**131**
Index		**137**

PREFACE

This book explores issues of race in regard to establishing a viable system of foster care for today's African American youth. Thirty-three states have cited high rates of poverty among African Americans as a factor influencing children's entry into foster care. African American children also stay in foster care longer, in part, because of a greater reliance on relatives to provide foster care. While states viewed some federal policies as helpful for reducing the proportion of African American children in foster care, they also expressed concerns regarding policies that limit the use of federal funds for services to prevent the removal of children in the first place and to place children with legal guardians. States also expressed concerns that federal funding emphasized finding permanent homes for children after they had been removed. This book aims to resolve the difficult issues of establishing new guidelines for foster care in the unique cases of so many African American children. This book consists of public domain documents which have been located, gathered, combined, reformatted, and enhanced with a subject index, selectively edited and bound to provide easy access.

Chapter 1 - A significantly greater proportion of African American children are in foster care than children of other races and ethnicities relative to their share of the general population. Given this situation, GAO was asked to analyze the (1) major factors influencing their proportion in foster care, (2) strategies states and localities have implemented that appear promising, and (3) ways in which federal policies may have influenced the proportion of African American children in foster care. This testimony is based on a GAO report issued in July 2007 (GAO-07-816), which included a nationwide survey; a review of research and policies; state site visits; analyses of child welfare data; and interviews with researchers, HHS officials, and other experts. It includes updates where possible.

Chapter 2 - Providing health care services for foster children, who often have significant health care needs, can be challenging. The Administration for Children and Families (ACF) oversees foster care, but state child welfare agencies are responsible for ensuring that these children receive health care services, which are often financed by Medicaid. In light of concerns about the health care needs of foster children, GAO was asked to study states' efforts to improve foster children's receipt of health services. This chapter has four objectives. It describes specific actions that some states have taken to (1) identify health care needs, (2) ensure delivery of appropriate health services, and (3) document and monitor the health care of children in foster care. It also describes the related technical assistance ACF offers to states.

To address these objectives, GAO selected 10 states and interviewed state officials and reviewed related documentation regarding the nature and results of the states' practices. To describe ACF's technical assistance, GAO interviewed officials and reviewed documents from ACF, states, and relevant technical assistance centers.

Chapter 3 - Congress passed the Foster Care Independence Act of 1999 (FCIA), which doubled annual federal funds for independent living programs to $140 million. This testimony discusses (1) states' FCIA funding allocations, (2) services provided and remaining challenges, (3) state coordination of programs to deliver services, and (4) the states and the Department of Health and Human Services' (HHS) Administration for Children and Families' (ACF) progress toward meeting program accountability requirements. This testimony is primarily based on our 2004 report on FCIA (05-25), with updated information from our 2007 testimony on state child welfare challenges (07-850T). To conduct the 2004 work, we surveyed state independent living coordinators, conducted 4 state site visits, and reviewed states' plans and annual reports. Updated information from our 2007 testimony was taken primarily from a 2006 survey of state child welfare directors.

Chapter 4 - The Child Welfare League of America represents hundreds of state and local child welfare organizations including both public and private, and faith-based agencies. CWLA members provide a range of child welfare services from prevention to placement services including adoptions, foster care, kinship placements, and services provided in a residential setting. CWLA's vision is that every child will grow up in a safe, loving, and stable family and that we will lead the nation in building public will to realize this vision.

Chapters 5 and 6 feature testimony before the U. S. House of Representatives.

Chapter 7 features charts and information on foster care and adoption.

In: Foster Care and African-American Youth ISBN: 978-1-60741-541-1
Editor: Joanna Kaczmarek

Chapter 1

AFRICAN AMERICAN CHILDREN IN FOSTER CARE: HHS AND CONGRESSIONAL ACTIONS COULD HELP REDUCE PROPORTION IN CARE*

United States Government Accountability Office

WHY GAO DID THIS STUDY

A significantly greater proportion of African American children are in foster care than children of other races and ethnicities relative to their share of the general population. Given this situation, GAO was asked to analyze the (1) major factors influencing their proportion in foster care, (2) strategies states and localities have implemented that appear promising, and (3) ways in which federal policies may have influenced the proportion of African American children in foster care. This testimony is based on a GAO report issued in July 2007 (GAO-07-816), which included a nationwide survey; a review of research and policies; state site visits; analyses of child welfare data; and interviews with researchers, HHS officials, and other experts. It includes updates where possible.

---

* This is an edited, reformatted and augmented version of a U. S. Government Accountability Office publication dated July 2008.

WHAT GAO RECOMMENDS

In our July 2007 report, GAO recommended that HHS further assist states in addressing disproportionality. HHS noted that GAO's recommendation was consistent with its efforts to provide technical assistance to states, but it has not addressed the specific actions. GAO continues to believe that further assistance is important for helping states address disproportionality. GAO also suggested that Congress consider amending current law to allow subsidies for legal guardianships. HHS believes its proposal for restructuring child welfare funding, first offered in 2004, would give states the option to do this, but the viability of this proposal is uncertain.

WHAT GAO FOUND

According to our survey results, key factors contributing to the proportion of African American children in foster care included a higher rate of poverty, challenges in accessing support services, racial bias and distrust, and difficulties in finding appropriate adoptive homes. Families living in poverty have greater difficulty accessing housing, mental health, and other support services needed to keep families stable and children safely at home. Bias or cultural misunderstandings and distrust between child welfare decision makers and the families they serve also contribute to children's removal from their homes into foster care. African American children also stay in foster care longer because of difficulties in recruiting adoptive parents, the lack of services for parents trying to reunify with their children, and a greater reliance on relatives to provide foster care who may be unwilling to terminate the parental rights of the child's parent—as required in adoption—or who need the financial subsidy they receive while the child is in foster care.

Most states we surveyed reported using various strategies intended to address these issues, such as building community supports, providing cultural competency training for caseworkers, and broadening the search for relatives to care for children. Researchers and officials also stressed the importance of analyzing data to address the proportion of African American children in care in order to better understand the issue and devise strategies to address it. HHS provides information and technical assistance, but states reported that they had limited capacity to analyze their own data and formulate strategies to address disproportionality.

According to our survey, states viewed some federal policies, such as those that promote adoption, as helpful for reducing the proportion of African American children in foster care. However, they also expressed concerns regarding policies that limit the use of federal funds to provide preventive services and support legal guardianship arrangements. As an alternative to adoption, subsidized guardianship is considered particularly promising for helping African American children exit from foster care.

Mr. Chairman and Members of the Subcommittee:

I am pleased to be here today to discuss our work on African American children and the extent to which they are disproportionately represented in foster care relative to their share of the general population.[1] Nationwide, about 510,000 children were in foster care at the end of fiscal year 2006, a significant proportion of them African American children. African American children were about three times as likely to be placed in foster care compared with White children in 2006, and African American children remained in foster care about 9 months longer as well.[2] This disproportionality occurs despite the fact that national studies have shown that children suffer from abuse and neglect at the same rates regardless of their race or ethnicity.[3] Although states vary considerably, data from nearly all states show some overrepresentation of African American children in foster care.

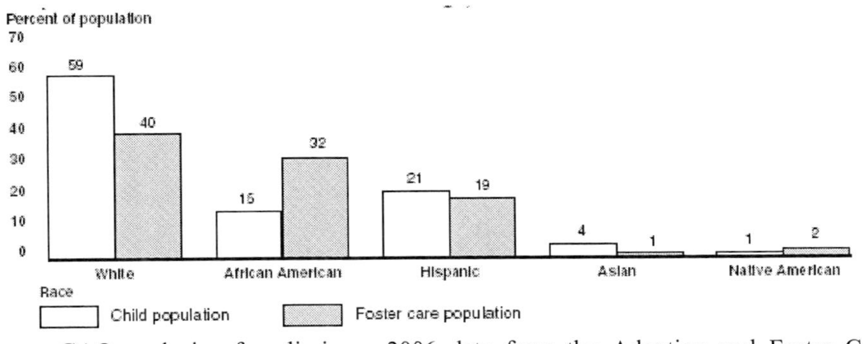

Source: GAO analysis of preliminary 2006 data from the Adoption and Foster Care Analysis and Reporting System and 2006 Census data.

Proportion of Children in Foster Care Settings, End of Fiscal Year 2006

As you know, about 60 percent of children who enter foster care do so in response to reports of child abuse or neglect that are provided to a state's child welfare system by doctors, teachers, police officers, and others.[4] Child welfare staff make decisions about whether a child can or cannot remain safely at home with their families, which are then presented before a judge who corroborates or overturns the decision. If a child enters foster care, child welfare staff develop case plans, approved by the courts, outlining the actions that parents must take before a child can be returned home. If the courts decide that children cannot be safely returned home, caseworkers establish other goals for them, such as adoption or legal guardianship. Although states have the primary responsibility for establishing the structures and programs of their child welfare services, federal policies establish a framework within which states make their programmatic and fiscal decisions. The Department of Health and Human Services (HHS) is the principal federal agency that provides federal oversight of states' child welfare systems.

My remarks today will focus on the following issues with regard to the proportion of African American children in foster care:

(1) The major factors that have been identified as influencing the proportion of African American children entering and remaining in foster care;
(2) the strategies that states and localities have implemented that appear promising in addressing African American children's overrepresentation in foster care; and
(3) the ways in which key federal child welfare policies[5] may have influenced African American children's representation in foster care.

This testimony is based on findings from our July 2007 report[6] on this subject, which we developed using multiple methodologies, including a nationwide Web-based survey of state child welfare administrators,[7] site visits to multiple states and counties, and interviews with child welfare researchers and HHS officials.[8] For our 2007 report, we also analyzed HHS data on foster care and adoption, conducted a review of research on racial disproportionality in foster care, and analyzed federal legislation and policies. For this testimony, we updated some information based on foster care and adoption data sources, but HHS did not provide us with any updates on its activities in time for this testimony. We conducted our work between June 2006 and July 2007 and updated as possible in July 2008 in accordance with generally accepted government auditing standards. Those standards require that we plan and perform the audit to obtain sufficient, appropriate evidence to provide a reasonable basis for our findings and conclusions based on our audit objectives. We believe that the evidence obtained provides a reasonable basis for our findings and conclusions based on our audit objectives.

SUMMARY

A higher rate of poverty and challenges in accessing support services, as well as racial bias coupled with distrust of the child welfare system, and difficulties in finding appropriate permanent homes were identified in our survey of child welfare directors as key factors influencing the proportion of African American children in foster care. Thirty-three states in our survey cited high rates of poverty among African Americans as a factor influencing children's entry into foster care. Also, families living in impoverished neighborhoods often do not have access to support services that can help them weather problems when they arise. However, research suggests that poverty does not fully account for differing rates of entry into foster care. State child welfare directors we surveyed also responded that bias or cultural misunderstanding and distrust between child welfare decision makers and the families they serve also contribute to the removal of children from their homes. For children who cannot be reunified with their families, state officials reported difficulties in finding them appropriate permanent homes, in part, because of the challenges in recruiting adoptive parents, especially for youth who are older or have special needs. African American children also stay in foster care longer, in part, because of a greater reliance on relatives to provide foster care. Although this type of foster care placement, known as kinship care, can be less traumatic for children, it is also associated with longer lengths of stay.

Researchers and officials stressed that no single strategy would fully address the issue of disproportionality, and most states in our survey reported implementing some strategies that experts have identified as promising for African American children. For example, some states are working to reduce bias by providing cultural competency training for caseworkers and to increase access to support services by collaborating with neighborhood-based support organizations. States also reported that they were working to increase the availability of permanent homes by diligently searching for fathers and other paternal kin who could provide care. However, public and private officials in the forefront of research and implementation said that the ability to analyze data was fundamental to any attempt to address racial disproportionality. State child welfare directors generally reported in our survey that they needed additional support in analyzing data on disproportionality and disseminating strategies. Our

July 2007 report therefore recommended that the Secretary of HHS provide states with additional technical assistance and tools to develop strategies to address disproportionality. In its comments, HHS noted that our recommendation was consistent with its efforts to provide technical assistance to states for addressing disproportionality, but the department did not address the specific actions we recommended. We continue to believe that it is important for HHS to take these actions to help states address this complex issue.

Finally, while states viewed some federal policies as helpful for reducing the proportion of African American children in foster care, they also expressed concerns regarding policies that limit the use of federal funds for services to prevent the removal of children in the first place and to place children with legal guardians. First, states expressed concerns that federal funding emphasized finding permanent homes for children after they had been removed, rather than on preventing the removal of children from their homes in the first place. With regard to finding homes for children who had already been removed, states generally viewed federal adoption policies as helpful in reducing disproportionality, including federal subsidies for adoptive families and the requirement to recruit minority adoptive parents. However, states faced challenges in recruiting enough adoptive parents. States also considered legal guardianship as particularly helpful in enabling African American children to exit foster care, but noted that while they can use federal funds to pay subsidies to adoptive parents, they cannot do so for legal guardians. Our draft report recommended that HHS pursue specific measures to allow adoption assistance payments to be used for subsidizing legal guardianship. In its comments, HHS disagreed with our recommendation, stating that its proposal for restructuring child welfare funding would give states the option to do this. However, HHS has presented this option in its budget proposal each year since 2004, but no legislation has been offered to date to authorize it. Because the viability of HHS's proposal is uncertain, in our July 2007 report we suggested that Congress consider amending current law to allow subsidies for legal guardianships. To date, the House of Representatives has passed a bill with a provision to allow states to use federal funds to subsidize legal guardianship for relatives, and the Senate has introduced a bill with a similar provision.

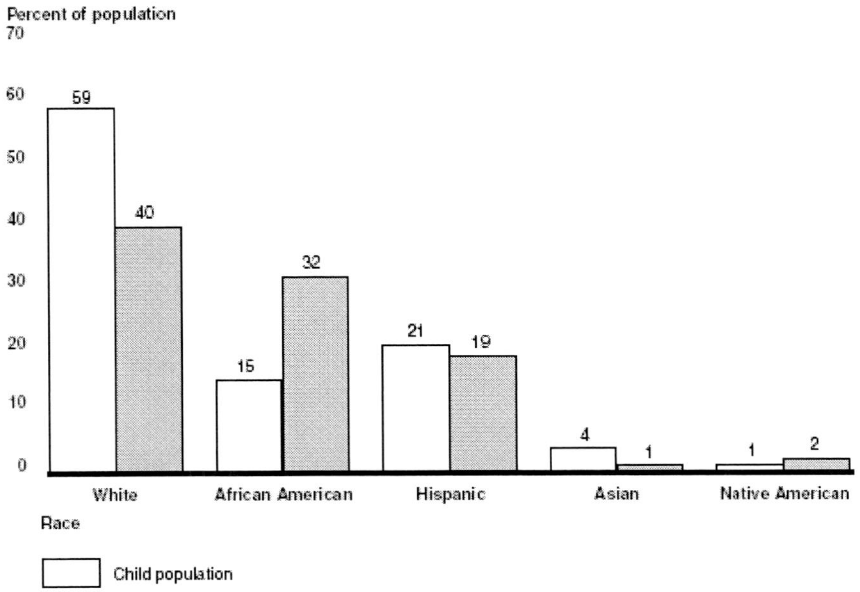

Source: GAO analysis of preliminary 2006 data from the Adoption and Foster Care Analysis and Reporting System and 2006 Census data.

Figure 1. Proportion of Children by Race in Foster Care Settings, End of Fiscal 2006

BACKGROUND

African American children were more likely to be placed in foster care than White or Hispanic children in 2006, and at each decision point in the child welfare process the disproportionality of African American children grows. Nationally, although African American children made up less than 15 percent of the overall child population in the 2000 Census, they represented 26 percent of the children who entered foster care during fiscal year 2006 and 32 percent of the children remaining in foster care at the end of that year (see Figure 1).[9]

There are various options for placing children in temporary and permanent homes through the child welfare system. Temporary options include foster care with relatives or nonrelatives—whether licensed or unlicensed—and group residential settings. According to HHS, approximately one-fourth of the children in out-of-home care are living with relatives, and this proportion is higher for Hispanic and African American families. For permanent placements, children can be reunified with their parents, or if reunification is not considered possible, children can be adopted or live with a legal guardian. Although both adoption and guardianship are considered permanent placement options under federal law,[10] an important difference is that adoption entails terminating parental rights, while guardianship does not. Another difference is that some adoptions may be subsidized with federal funds.

Federal funds account for approximately half of states' total reported spending for child welfare services, with the rest of funding coming from states and localities. In fiscal year 2004, total federal spending on child welfare was estimated to be $11.7 billion based on analysis of data from more than 40 states.[11] Titles IV-E and IV-B of the Social Security Act are the principal sources of federal funds dedicated for child welfare activities. Title IV-E supports payments to foster families, subsidies for families who provide adoptive homes to children who states identify as having special needs that make placement difficult,[12] and related administrative costs on behalf of children who meet federal eligibility criteria. Title IV-E payments for foster care maintenance are open-ended entitlements. Title IV-B authorizes funds to states for broad child welfare purposes, including child protection, family preservation, and adoption services; these funds are appropriated annually.[13] Federal block grants, such as the Temporary Assistance for Needy Families (TANF) and the Social Services Block Grant (SSBG), provide additional sources of funds that states can use for child welfare purposes. States have discretion to provide direct social services for various populations, including child welfare families, the elderly, and people with disabilities.

In 1994, the Congress authorized the use of demonstration waivers to encourage innovative and effective child welfare practices. These waivers, typically authorized for 5 years, allowed states to use Title IV-E funds to provide services and supports other than foster care maintenance payments. For example, four states had completed demonstrations that involved subsidized guardianships, and, as of May 2007, seven states had active guardianship demonstrations and one state had not yet implemented its guardianship demonstration. Demonstration waivers must remain cost-neutral to the federal government, and they must undergo rigorous program evaluation to determine their effectiveness.

STATES REPORT POVERTY AND DIFFICULTY IN FINDING PERMANENT HOMES ARE AMONG MAJOR FACTORS INFLUENCING AFRICAN AMERICANS ENTRY AND LENGTH OF STAY

A complex set of interrelated factors influence the disproportionate number of African American children who enter foster care, as well as their longer lengths of stay. Major factors affecting children's entry into foster care included African American families' higher rates of poverty, difficulties in accessing support services, and racial bias or cultural misunderstanding among child welfare decision makers, as well as families' distrust of the child welfare system. Factors often cited as affecting African American children's length of stay in foster care included the lack of appropriate adoptive homes for children, parents' lack of access to support services needed for reunification with their children, and a greater use of kinship care among African American families. (See figure 2.)

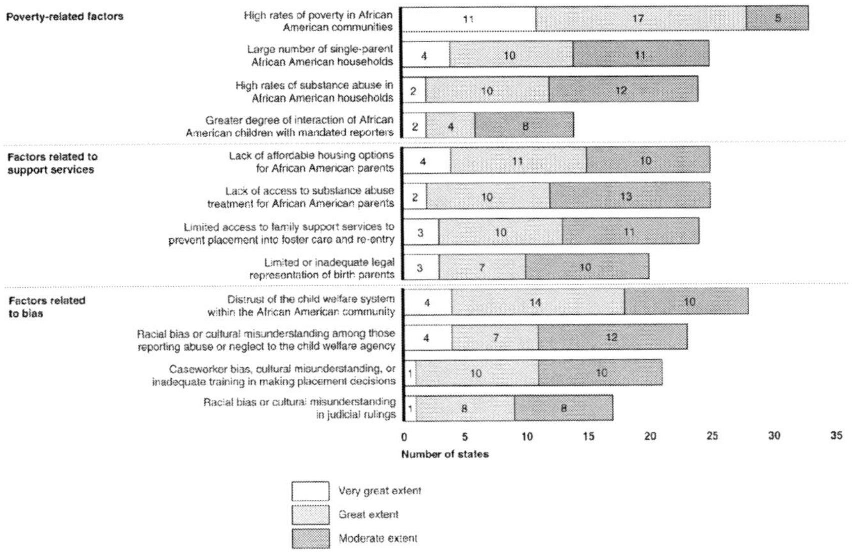

Source: GAO analysis of state child welfare survey responses.

Figure 2. State Views of Factors Affecting Higher Entry of African American Children to Foster Care

In our survey, 33 of the 48 states from which we received responses reported that high rates of poverty in African American communities and issues related to living in poverty may increase the proportion of African American children entering foster care compared to that of children of other races and ethnicities. Across the nation, African American families were nearly four times more likely to live in poverty than White families, according to U.S. Census data.[14] Since foster care programs primarily serve children from low-income families, this could account for some of the disproportionate number of African American children in the foster care system. In addition, child welfare directors in 25 states reported that the greater number of African American single-parent households contributed to African American children's entry into foster care. According to the most recent National Incidence Study, children of single parents, who are also more likely than married couples to be poor, had a 77 to 87 percent greater risk of harm than children from two-parent families.[15] Across the nation, 34 percent of African American family households with children under 18 years of age were headed by single females compared to 9 percent for Whites and 19 percent for Hispanics, according to U.S. Census data.[16]

Moreover, families living in impoverished neighborhoods often do not have access to the kinds of supports and services that can prevent problems in the home from leading to abuse or neglect, according to states we surveyed and other research. Such supports and services include affordable and adequate housing; substance abuse treatment; access to family services such as parenting skills workshops and counseling; and adequate legal representation.[17] Also, there is some evidence that African American families, in particular, are not offered the same amount of support services when they are brought to the attention of the child welfare system.[18]

Coupled with African American parents' greater distrust of the child welfare system, racial bias or cultural misunderstanding among decision makers also emerged in our survey as major factors contributing to the disproportionate number of African American children entering foster care. According to state child welfare officials and some researchers we interviewed, African American families' distrust of the child welfare system stems from their perception that the system is unresponsive to their needs and racially biased against them. This perception can shape the families' dynamics in their initial contacts with mandated reporters, caseworkers, and judges, which can increase the risk the child will be removed from the home. In our survey, state child welfare directors also reported that they considered racial bias or cultural misunderstanding on the part of those reporting abuse or neglect—such as teachers, medical professionals, or police officers, as well as among caseworkers—as factors in the disproportionate representation of African American children entering foster care. In support of this view, some studies have found that medical professionals are more likely to report low-income or minority children to child protective services.[19] Although research on racial bias or race as a predictor for entry into foster care is not always consistent, a recent review of the current research concluded that race is an important factor that affects the decision to place children into foster care.[20]

Among factors cited as affecting African American children's longer lengths of stay in foster care, officials from 29 states cited an insufficient number of appropriate adoptive homes as a key factor. African American children constituted nearly half of the children legally available for adoption in 2004, and they waited significantly longer than other children for an adoptive placement. Factors that make finding adoptive families for African American children challenging include the difficulty many states have in recruiting adoptive families of the same race and ethnicity as the children waiting for adoption and the unwillingness of some families to adopt a child of another race. In addition, states we surveyed reported that African American children waiting to be adopted were older, and prospective adoptive parents are more inclined to adopt younger children.[21] (See figure 3.)

Additionally, the belief that African American children are more likely to be diagnosed as having medical and other special needs, which may contribute to their longer lengths of stay in foster care, was reported by state officials. In fact, African American children in foster care in 2004 were only slightly more likely to have been diagnosed as having medical conditions or other disabilities (28 percent) than White children in foster care (26 percent), according to HHS data. However, 23 percent of African American children who were adopted out of foster care had a medical condition or disability, compared to 31 percent of White children in the same category.

Some of the same factors that states view as contributing to African American children's entry also contribute to their difficulties in exiting foster care and being reunified with their families. In our survey, nearly half of the states considered the lack of affordable housing, distrust of the child welfare system, and lack of substance abuse treatment as factors contributing to African American children's longer lengths of stay. The lack of such supports and other services in many poor African American neighborhoods contributes to children's longer stays in foster care because services can influence a parent's ability to reunify with their child in a timely manner, according to our survey, interviews, and research.

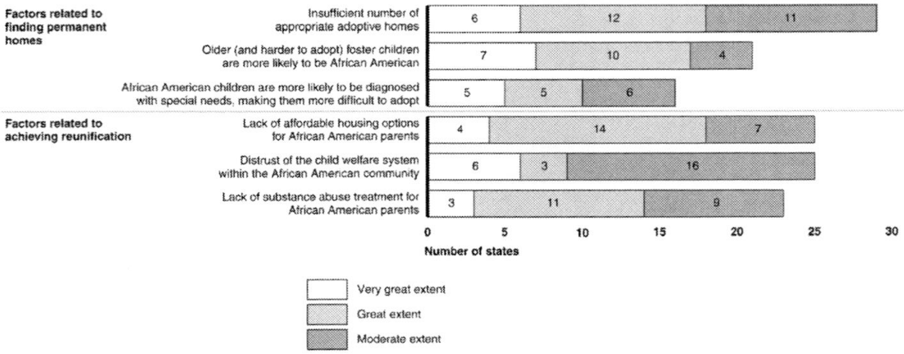

Source: GAO analysis of state child welfare survey responses.

Figure 3. State Views of Factors Affecting Longer Time in Foster Care for African American Children

States also reported that the use of kinship care was a factor contributing to longer lengths of stay in foster care for African American children. African American children are more likely than White and Asian children to enter into the care of relatives, which is associated with longer lengths of stay. Relatives may be unwilling to adopt the child because it would require termination of their relative's parental rights or because they might lose needed financial support they receive as foster parents. However, despite the longer lengths of stay, child welfare researchers and officials we interviewed consider these placements to be positive options for African American children because they are less stressful to the child and maintain familial ties.

States Reported Implementing Strategies Considered Promising for Addressing Disproportionality but Also Reported Needing More Technical Assistance

Researchers and child welfare administrators we interviewed stressed that no single strategy could fully address disproportionality in foster care, partly because so many interrelated factors contribute to it. According to our survey, the strategies that states implemented tended to focus on addressing racial and cultural bias in decision making, families' problems in accessing support services, and agencies' challenges in finding permanent homes so that children can exit foster care more quickly. In addition, data collection and analysis were considered essential for identifying problems and devising strategies to address them, but states reported needing additional assistance in this area.

To help mitigate bias and cultural misunderstanding among decision makers, states reported implementing a range of strategies, such as including family members in case planning; providing training to strengthen caseworkers' competency in working with families from various cultures; reaching out to ensure that public officials are not inappropriately referring families for abuse and neglect through mandated reporting; and implementing the use of certain tools to help caseworkers make more systematic decisions regarding the level of a child's risk. (See figure 4.) According to an evaluation in Texas, for example, for African American families who participated in case planning that included family group decision making, 32 percent of the children returned home—more than twice as many as in families who received traditional services.

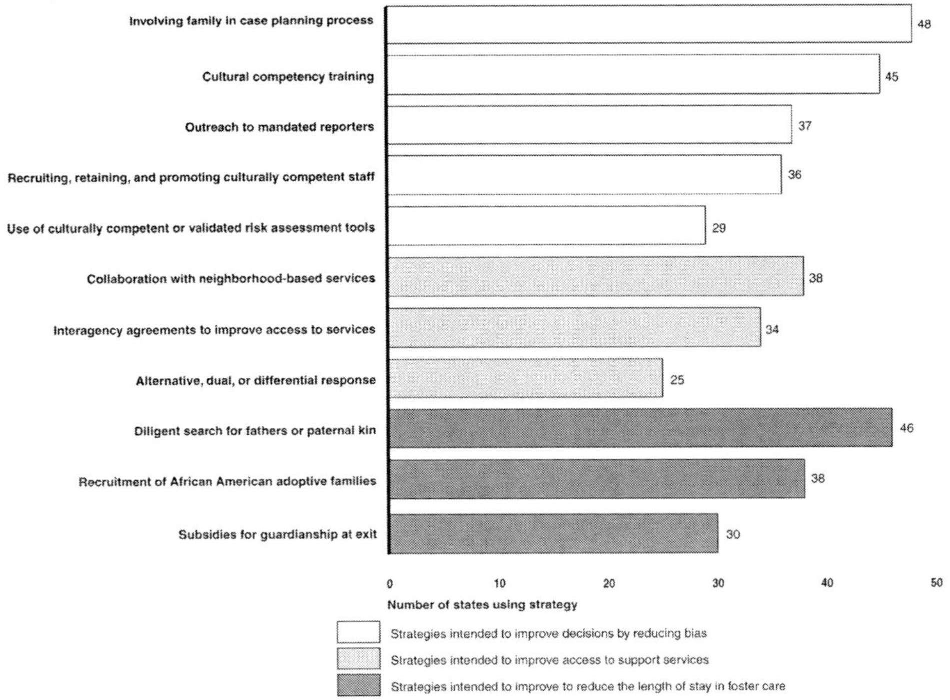

Source: GAO analysis of state child welfare survey responses.

Figure 4. Number of States Using Strategies to Address Disproportionality, Grouped by Type of Factor

To improve families' access to services, states reported collaborating with neighborhood-based support organizations, establishing interagency agreements to improve access to these services, and implementing an alternative approach to the assessment process that emphasizes helping families obtain needed supports and services, instead of removing children from their families. For example, in Los Angeles County, child welfare officials went door to door in minority neighborhoods to find service providers beyond those with whom they historically contracted. This collaboration helped build trust between the community and the child welfare agency and increased families' use of the services provided.

For African American children who cannot ultimately be reunified with their parents, states also reported devising strategies to increase the number of permanent homes available to them. To increase the options for African American children, 46 states reported making diligent searches for fathers and other paternal kin who can care for these children—not a routine practice until recently. Additionally, a federal law passed in 1994 and amended in 1996 require states to diligently recruit potential foster and adoptive families that reflect the ethnic and racial diversity of children in the state who need foster and adoptive homes.[22] Likely in response to these laws, states have adopted various strategies to recruit greater numbers of African American adoptive parents, such as contracting with faith-based organizations and convening adoption support teams. However, despite these efforts, the number of African American children adopted by African American parents has not increased in recent years. In addition, HHS's 2001 to 2004 review found that only 21 of 52 states were sufficiently recruiting minority families, and one report found that the recruitment of minority families was one of the greatest challenges for nearly all states.[23]

Using subsidized guardianship as an alternative to adoption may hold particular promise for reducing disproportionality, and more than half of the states surveyed reported using this strategy.[24] African American children are more likely than White children to be placed with relatives for foster care, which is generally a longer-term placement, and these relative caregivers are also more likely than nonrelative foster parents to be low-income. They may be unwilling to adopt because they may find it difficult financially to forego foster care payments or because adoption entails terminating the parental rights of their kin. However, subsidized guardianship programs provide financial support for foster parents (often relatives) who agree to become legally responsible for children but are unable or willing to adopt. When Illinois and California implemented two of the largest of such programs, they subsequently saw an increase in permanent placements for all children. After instituting their subsidized guardianship programs, more than 40 percent of children who were in long-term relative foster care in both states found permanency. In Illinois, this decrease also coincided with a reduction in disproportionate numbers of African American children in foster care.

In addition to these types of strategies, child welfare administrators and researchers told us that data collection, analysis, and dissemination are needed to inform attempts to address disproportionality. These data can include not only disproportionality rates but also information that identifies the extent to which disproportionality occurs among different age groups, at different stages in the child welfare process, and in different locations. For example, a California researcher used state data to show that African American infants enter foster care at a much higher rate than infants of other races or ethnicities and that this disproportionality grows as children get older because African American children are also less likely to exit foster care. Such data analyses help states and localities devise strategies to address the issue and can also be useful for building consensus among community leaders and policymakers for action. However, some state and local agencies have limited capacity to do this. In responding to our survey, 25 states reported that receiving technical assistance from HHS in calculating disproportionality rates and tracking it over time would be useful.[25] California state child welfare officials told us that without the aid of a university researcher, they would not have the ability to help counties that lack the capacity to collect and analyze their data. Despite the importance of data analysis, 18 states reported that they were not regularly analyzing or using data in their efforts to address disproportionality.

HHS has made technical assistance and information on disproportionality available to states at conferences and through various HHS Web sites. In addition, the agency is compiling an inventory of tools and best practices for addressing disproportionality. Despite these efforts, states report that they need further information and technical assistance to strengthen their current efforts in addressing disproportionality. Accordingly, in our July 2007 report, we recommended that HHS take certain actions to further assist states in understanding and addressing the nature and extent of racial disproportionality in their child welfare systems. In its comments, HHS noted that our recommendation was consistent with its efforts to provide technical assistance to states for addressing disproportionality, but the department did not address the specific actions we recommended. We continue to believe that it is important for HHS to take these actions to help states address this complex issue.

States Reported That More Flexibility to Use Federal Funds for Prevention Services and Subsidized Guardianship Could Help Reduce Disproportionality

While states viewed some federal policies as helpful for reducing the proportion of African American children in foster care, they also expressed concerns regarding policies that limit the use of federal funds to provide preventive services and support legal guardianship arrangements. As an alternative to adoption, states considered subsidized guardianship as particularly helpful in enabling African American children to exit foster care but noted that while they can use federal child welfare funds to pay subsidies to adoptive parents, they cannot do so for guardians.[26]

At least half the states we surveyed noted that the structure of federal child welfare funding may contribute to disproportionality by favoring foster care placements over services to prevent the removal of children from their homes in the first place. Of particular concern to 28 states in our survey were the caps on funding for preventive and family support services under Title IV-B, and 25 states expressed concern about their inability to use foster care funds under Title IV-E for purposes other than making payments to foster care families. A recent GAO report similarly found that preventive and family support services were the services most in need of greater federal, state, or local resources.[27] According to California and Minnesota officials, because the majority of federal child welfare funds are used for foster care payments instead of preventive services, federal funding policies did not align with states' efforts to reduce the number of children entering foster care by serving at-risk children safely in their homes. However, states do have the freedom to use other federal funds, particularly TANF block grants, to provide preventive and supportive services to families, and 23 states reported that the ability to use these funds contributes to a reduction in the proportion of African American children in foster care.[28] States face competing priorities for the use of their TANF block grant funds, and not all states use them for child welfare activities.

Once children are removed, states reported that federal policies promoting adoption were generally helpful; however, states' views were mixed on certain requirements specifically intended to eliminate race-related barriers to adoption. Policies that promote adoption of African American children were generally viewed as helpful, such as allowing states to classify African American children as having "special needs," which allows them to provide subsidies to adoptive parents, according to our survey results. However, views of other requirements were mixed. Although 22 states reported that the federal policies requiring states to diligently recruit ethnically and racially diverse adoptive families would help reduce disproportionality, 9 states reported the federal requirements had no effect, and 15 states reported that they were unable to tell.[29]

States continue to face challenges in recruiting adoptive families—such as a shortage of willing and qualified parents, especially for older African American children, or a lack of resources for recruiting initiatives—and more than half of states are not meeting HHS performance goals in this area.[30] Over the last 5 years, African American children and Native American children have consistently experienced lower rates of adoption than children of other races and ethnicities, and since 2000, adoption rates have reached a plateau, according to HHS data and other research.

As an alternative to adoption, many child welfare officials and researchers we interviewed considered subsidizing legal guardianship a particularly important way to help African American children exit foster care. However, there are no federal subsidies for guardianship similar to those available for adoption, which constrains states' ability to place children in these arrangements. Seven states have a federal demonstration waiver, which allows them to use Title IV-E funds for subsidized guardianship. All states did so in a cost-neutral manner, as required by the waivers.[31] In California and Illinois, subsidizing these legal guardianships has been found to reduce the number of children in foster care, including African American children. In addition, guardianship and adoption both have been found to provide comparable levels of stability for children and show similar outcomes in terms of emotional and physical health, according to an evaluation of Illinois's guardianship program. Because of the challenges states face finding adoptive homes for many African American children and because legal guardianship may offer a more suitable alternative for families who want to permanently care for related children without necessarily adopting them, we recommended, in our 2007 draft report, that HHS pursue specific measures to allow adoption assistance payments to be used for subsidizing legal guardianship. In its comments, HHS disagreed with our recommendation, stating that its proposal for restructuring child welfare funding, known as the Child Welfare Program Option, would give states the option to do this. However, HHS has presented this option in its budget proposal each year since 2004, but no legislation has been offered to date to authorize it. Moreover, even if enacted, it is unknown how many states would choose to implement this funding structure. Because the viability of HHS's proposal is uncertain, in our final July 2007 report, we suggested that Congress consider amending current law to allow adoption assistance payments to be used for legal guardianship. To date, the House of Representatives has passed a bill with a provision to allow states to use federal funds to subsidize legal guardianship for relatives, and the Senate has introduced a bill with a similar provision.

Mr. Chairman, this concludes my statement. I would be pleased to respond to any questions you or other Members of the Subcommittee may have.

RELATED GAO PRODUCTS

Disconnected Youth: Federal Action Could Address Some of the Challenges Faced by Local Programs That Reconnect Youth to Education and Employment. GAO-08-313. Washington, D.C.: February 28, 2008.

African American Children in Foster Care: Additional HHS Assistance Needed to Help States Reduce the Proportion in Care. GAO-07-816. Washington, D.C.: July 11, 2007.

Child Welfare: Improving Social Service program, Training, and Technical Assistance Information Would Help Address Long-standing Service-level and Workforce Challenges. GAO-07-75. Washington, D.C.: October 6, 2006.

Child and Family Services Reviews: Better Use of Data and Improved Guidance Could Enhance HHS's Oversight of State Performance. GAO-04-333. Washington, D.C.: April 20, 2004.

HHS Actions Could Improve Coordination of Services and Monitoring of States' Independent Living Programs. GAO-05-25. Washington, D.C.: November 18, 2004.

Child Welfare: Enhanced Federal Oversight of Title IV-B Could Provide States Additional Information to Improve Services. GAO-03-956. Washington, D.C.: September 12, 2003.

Child Welfare and Juvenile Justice: Federal Agencies Could Play a Stronger Role in Helping States Reduce the Number of Children Placed Solely to Obtain Mental Health Service. GAO-03-397. Washington, D.C.: April 23, 2003 (reissued on August 11, 2003).

Foster Care: Recent Legislation Helps States Focus on Finding Permanent Homes for Children, but Long-Standing Barriers Remain. GAO-02-585. Washington, D.C.: June 28, 2002.

Foster Care: Kinship Care Quality and Permanency Issues. GAO-99-32. Washington, D.C.: May 6, 1999.

Foster Care Implementation of the Multiethnic Placement Act Poses Difficult Challenges. GAO-98-204. Washington, D.C.: September 14, 1998.

End Notes

[1] Racial disproportionality refers to the extent that children of a certain race or ethnic group are over- or underrepresented in foster care relative to their proportion in the population.

[2] The difference in length of time in foster care is based on 2004 Adoption and Foster Care Analysis and Reporting System data because we were not able to obtain more recent data in time for this testimony.

[3] See the National Incidence Study (NIS), a congressionally mandated, periodic effort of the National Center on Child Abuse and Neglect to obtain information about the current incidence of child abuse and neglect in the United States. NIS-1 was published in 1981, NIS-2 in 1988, and NIS-3 in 1996. The NIS-3 findings are based on a nationally representative sample of over 5,600 professionals in 842 agencies serving 42 counties in the United States. Reports from the NIS-4 are anticipated in December 2008.

[4] Children also enter foster care for other reasons, such as their parents' illness, death, or disability or because of the children's delinquent behavior and truancy.

[5] We are using the term "policy" in this testimony to include federal laws, regulations, and informal agency guidance.

[6] GAO, *African American Children in Foster Care: Additional HHS Assistance Needed to Help States Reduce the Proportion in Care*, GAO-07-816 (Washington, D.C.: July 11, 2007).

[7] We surveyed the 50 states and the District of Columbia and received responses from 47 states and the District of Columbia.

[8] Although we focused on African American children in this testimony and our report, our report also noted points of similarity or difference with children of other races and ethnicities as appropriate. Native Americans are also overrepresented nationally, but some are affected by different child welfare laws and oversight authority than African Americans, making comparisons challenging. See GAO-07-816 for more information.

[9] Although racial disproportionality is most severe and pervasive for African American children, Native American children also experience higher rates of representation in foster care than children of other races or ethnicities. It is also important to understand local variations for Hispanic and Asian children, since they are underrepresented in foster care nationally and in most states but are overrepresented in some counties and states. For disproportionality rates for African American, White, Hispanic, Asian, and Native American children by state in fiscal year 2004, see appendix II of GAO-07-816.

[10] The Adoption and Safe Families Act of 1997 (Pub. L. No. 105-89) recognized legal guardianship under federal law as another option for placing children in permanent homes. Prior to this, children's options for exiting foster care included being reunified with their parents, adopted by a relative or nonrelative, or emancipated from foster care when they had reached a certain age, usually 18.

[11] These data were reported in the Urban Institute 2005 Child Welfare Survey in May 2006. This funding analysis is the most recent available that shows federal funding used specifically for child welfare.

[12] The term "special needs" is used in a distinct way in Title IV-E programs. In order to be considered a child with special needs for the purpose of providing adoption assistance payments, states must determine that the child should not return home and have a factor or condition that would make the child difficult to place for adoption without such payments. States are provided discretion under federal law to determine what these factors or conditions are and may include

age, membership in a sibling or minority group, or having a medical or developmental disability that would make placement difficult. There are additional eligibility requirements to obtain adoption assistance subsidies as well.

[13] For further information on Title IV-B funds, see GAO, *Child Welfare: Enhanced Federal Oversight of Title IV-B Could Provide States Additional Information to Improve Services*, GAO-03-956 (Washington, D.C.: Sept. 12, 2003).

[14] U.S. Census American Community Survey, 2006.

[15] A. Sedlak and D. Broadhurst, *Executive Summary of the Third National Incidence Study of Child Abuse and Neglect.* A report prepared for the U.S. Department of Health and Human Services, (Washington, D.C., 1996).

[16] U.S. Census American Community Survey data from 2006.

[17] Some child welfare officials also pointed out that lower income families may be referred to the child welfare system in order to gain access to such services.

[18] Ann F. Garland et al., "Racial and Ethnic Variations in Mental Health Care Utilization Among Children in Foster Care," *Children's Services: Social Policy, Research and Practice*, 3(3): 133-146 (2000).

[19] For example: R. L. Hampton and E. Newberger, "Child Abuse Incidence and Reporting by Hospitals: Significance of Severity, Class and Race," *American Journal of Public Health* (75) 1: 56-60 (1985). For information on other studies, see Robert Hill, *Synthesis of Research on Disproportionality in Child Welfare: An Update* (Casey–Center for the Study of Social Policy Alliance for Racial Equity in the Child Welfare System, 2006).

[20] Robert B. Hill, *Synthesis of Research on Disproportionality in Child Welfare: An Update* (Casey-Center for the Study of Social Policy Alliance for Racial Equity in the Child Welfare System, 2006).

[21] According to our analysis of Adoption and Foster Care Analysis and Reporting System (AFCARS) fiscal year 2004 data, African American children are even more disproportionally represented in foster care at older ages than other children.

[22] See the Multi-Ethnic Placement Act of 1994 (Pub. L. No. 103-382, §§ 551-553), as amended in 1996 by the Interethnic Adoption Provisions included in the Small Business Job Protection Act (Pub. L. No. 104-88, § 1808), referred to as MEPA/IEP.

[23] Urban Institute Child Welfare Research Program, *Foster Care Adoption in the United States: A State by State Analysis of Barriers and Promising Approaches* (November 2004).

[24] A 2006 report by Generations United found that a total of 35 states and the District of Columbia were subsidizing legal guardianships, generally through federal IV-E waivers; federal block grants, such as TANF; or state and local funds. (See http://ipath.gu.org/documents/A0/GU-GeneralFactSheetJune.pdf.) Three of these states, Maryland, New Jersey, and Rhode Island, did not respond to our survey on disproportionality. Other states may subsidize guardianships but not limit these subsidies to families involved in the state child welfare system.

[25] Although 18 states in our survey believed that having reporting requirements on disproportionality rates in HHS's Child and Family Services Review process would be useful, nearly as many responded that it would not be useful. HHS officials told us that this process was governed by statute and that they could not add such a requirement.

[26] As of May 2007, seven states that were granted waivers to use Title IV-E funds to provide services and supports other than foster care maintenance payments were actively using Title IV-E funds to provide subsidies for guardianships.

[27] See GAO, *Child Welfare: Improving Social Service program, Training, and Technical Assistance Information Would Help Address Long-standing Service-level and Workforce Challenges,* GAO-07-75 (Washington, D.C.: Oct. 6, 2006).

[28] As with all block grants, state officials determine the use of these funds and their program priorities.

[29] MEPA/IEP also prohibits foster care and adoption agencies receiving federal funds from delaying or denying placement decisions on the basis of race, color, or national origin. Fifteen states

reported that encouraging race-neutral adoptions would help reduce disproportionality, 18 states responded that this policy had no effect, and 12 states reported that they were unable to tell.

[30] This is based on HHS data from between 2001 and 2004. Challenges in recruiting are consistent with survey responses in an earlier GAO study as well. See GAO-07-75.

[31] According to HHS officials, these programs can be cost-neutral because the administrative costs associated with maintaining a child in foster care are no longer incurred with permanent legal guardianships.

In: Foster Care and African-American Youth
Editor: Joanna Kaczmarek
ISBN: 978-1-60741-541-1

Chapter 2

FOSTER CARE: STATE PRACTICES FOR ASSESSING HEALTH NEEDS, FACILITATING SERVICE DELIVERY, AND MONITORING CHILDREN'S CARE*

United States Government Accountability Office

WHY GAO DID THIS STUDY

Providing health care services for foster children, who often have significant health care needs, can be challenging. The Administration for Children and Families (ACF) oversees foster care, but state child welfare agencies are responsible for ensuring that these children receive health care services, which are often financed by Medicaid. In light of concerns about the health care needs of foster children, GAO was asked to study states' efforts to improve foster children's receipt of health services. This chapter has four objectives. It describes specific actions that some states have taken to (1) identify health care needs, (2) ensure delivery of appropriate health services, and (3) document and monitor the health care of children in foster care. It also describes the related technical assistance ACF offers to states.

* This is an edited, reformatted and augmented version of a U. S. Government Accountability Office publication dated February 2009.

To address these objectives, GAO selected 10 states and interviewed state officials and reviewed related documentation regarding the nature and results of the states' practices. To describe ACF's technical assistance, GAO interviewed officials and reviewed documents from ACF, states, and relevant technical assistance centers.

What GAO Recommends

GAO did not make any recommendations in this chapter. In commenting on this chapter, Health and Human Services provided additional information on its technical assistance efforts and technical comments which have been incorporated as appropriate.

What GAO Found

To identify the health needs of children entering foster care, all 10 states we studied have adopted policies that specify the timing and scope of children's health assessments, and some states use designated providers to conduct the assessments. All of the states we selected for study required physical examinations, most states we studied required mental health and developmental screens, and several of them required or recommended substance abuse screens for youth shortly after entry into foster care. Preventive health examinations for foster children were required at regular intervals thereafter, in line with states' Medicaid standards. Limited research has suggested that having assessment policies and using designated providers who have greater experience in the health needs of foster children may permit fuller identification and follow-up of children's health care needs.

To help ensure the delivery of appropriate health care services, states have adopted practices to facilitate access, coordinate care, and review medications for children in foster care. Some states used specialized staff to quickly determine Medicaid eligibility; others issued temporary Medicaid cards to prevent delays in obtaining treatment. In addition, certain states had increased payments to physicians serving children in foster care to encourage more physicians to provide needed care. Nurses or other health care managers were given roles in coordinating care to help ensure that children received necessary health care services. Six states we studied also reported monitoring the use of various medications, including psychotropic medications intended for the treatment of mental health disorders.

To document and monitor children's health care, several states we studied had shared data across state programs and employed quality assurance measures, such as medical audits, to track receipt of services. One state has developed a foster care health "passport" that electronically compiles data from multiple sources, including the state's immunization registry, and this passport can be accessed and updated by responsible parties through a secure Web site. Other states used electronic databases to obtain more complete and timely medical histories than otherwise available but provided more limited access to these and continued to update them through use of paper records.

ACF's network of 25 technical assistance centers is intended to improve state performance in meeting children's needs, including their health care needs, by increasing the capacity of state agencies to ensure safety, wellbeing, and availability of permanent homes for children in their care. According to ACF officials, the centers are not intended to provide medical expertise, but to help state child welfare agencies collaborate with others involved with health programs. One center in ACF's network focuses exclusively on children's mental health and several others have also assisted in identifying some practices to improve the health of children in foster care. Five of the centers are newly funded and are expected to provide long-term help in implementing plans to improve agency performance in meeting children's needs.

ABBREVIATIONS

AAP	American Academy of Pediatrics
ACF	Administration for Children and Families
AIDS	Acquired immune deficiency syndrome
CBO	Congressional Budget Office
CFSR	Child and Family Services Reviews
CMS	Centers for Medicare & Medicaid Services
EPSDT	Early and Periodic Screening, Diagnosis, and Treatment
HHS	Department of Health and Human Services
HIV	Human immunodeficiency virus
HRSA	Health Resources and Services Administration
PIP	Program improvement plan
SAMHSA	Substance Abuse and Mental Health Services Administration

SCHIP State Children's Health Insurance Program

February 6, 2009

The Honorable Jim McDermott
Chairman
Subcommittee on Income Security and Family Support
Committee on Ways and Means
House of Representatives

Dear Mr. Chairman:

Some of our nation's most vulnerable children are those who have been removed from their homes and placed in foster care, often due to abuse or neglect. Of the nearly 500,000 children in foster care at the end of fiscal year 2007, 80 percent are estimated to have significant health care needs, including chronic health conditions, developmental concerns, and mental health needs. Treatment for the health care needs of children in foster care is generally financed through states' Medicaid programs.[1] In addition to the extent of foster children's health care needs, the disruptions associated with foster care—such as having to leave home and experiencing several changes in placement—may increase the challenges of ensuring that these children receive health care services. However, conditions left untreated can impede children's ability to realize their potential or become self-sufficient later in life.

States are responsible for ensuring that children in foster care receive necessary health care services. The Administration for Children and Families (ACF) within the Department of Health and Human Services (HHS) provides funding for state child welfare programs, including foster care. In exchange for this funding, states agree to meet basic federal requirements.[2] However, they also have flexibility in how they design and implement their programs. In its past reviews of state agencies' performance, ACF determined that children under agency supervision, including those in foster care, may not all receive appropriate physical or mental health care services. For example, ACF found that about 30 percent of children sampled either did not have their health needs assessed or did not receive treatment during the period reviewed. In these cases, states were required to develop and implement improvement plans, and ACF monitored their implementation.

In October 2008, Congress expanded the federal requirements related to foster children by mandating that states explicitly plan for the ongoing oversight and coordination of health care services for children in foster care.[3] The state practices described in this chapter, although in use before the expansion of federal requirements, address some of the new requirements and, thus, may be helpful to other states as they consider changes in their plans. Specifically, this chapter addresses four objectives. It describes practices that selected states have adopted to address the challenges of (1) identifying health care needs, (2) ensuring delivery of appropriate health services, and (3) documenting and monitoring the health care of children in foster care. In addition, the report describes the technical assistance that ACF offers states to help improve their performance in providing for the health care needs of these children.[4]

To address these objectives, we selected 10 states for in-depth study based on the information they provided and the variations they represented in geographic location, foster care caseload, and child welfare administrative structures. The 10 states selected were California, Delaware, Florida, Illinois, Massachusetts, New York, Oklahoma, Texas, Utah, and Washington. (For more information on our state selection, see appendix I.) We conducted site visits in three of these states to describe state practices in context and gather views of multiple stakeholders, such as state child welfare officials, health or Medicaid officials, health care providers, foster parents, and in two cases (Cook County, Illinois and New York City), the views of child welfare personnel in major metropolitan areas. In our interviews with officials of the seven remaining states, conducted by telephone, we focused primarily on interviewing child welfare and Medicaid officials regarding certain practices that state agencies identified.[5] We cannot generalize the results of our review from the 10 states we selected to all states. Although we did not examine the actual operation of every practice, we reviewed information about states' practices through such means as discussions with researchers, advocates, and other parties who had knowledge of these states' foster care programs and, where available, we also collected and evaluated research, state data, and other information on the effectiveness of the practices adopted. In addition, we reviewed relevant federal laws, policies, and guidance and research literature on the physical and mental health needs and treatment of children in foster care. To obtain information on ACF's provision of technical assistance, we reviewed documents and interviewed officials at ACF and six centers participating in ACF's network of technical assistance providers, including the two centers jointly funded by ACF and HHS's Substance Abuse and Mental Health Services Administration (SAMHSA). Our work was designed to describe specific state and federal practices, not to assess compliance with statutory or regulatory requirements. We conducted our work from November 2007 to January 2009, in accordance with all sections of GAO's Quality Assurance Framework that are relevant to our objectives. The framework requires that we plan and perform the engagement to obtain sufficient and appropriate evidence to meet our stated objectives and to discuss any limitations in our work. We believe that the information and data obtained, and the analysis conducted, provide a reasonable basis for any findings and conclusions.

RESULTS IN BRIEF

To identify the health needs of children, the states we studied generally reported adopting policies that specified the timing and scope of children's health assessments and, in some cases, also employed designated providers to conduct these assessments. These assessment features were intended to increase the likelihood of more complete identification and follow-up of children's needs. Although ACF had not imposed specific requirements for health assessments, the 10 states we selected for study required that children have a general physical—often referred to as a well-child exam—within 30 days of entering foster care, in line with recommendations from professional associations. Most of these states also required that children's mental health and developmental status be screened after entry, and several of the states we selected for study cited screening for substance abuse. The 10 states also required preventive health examinations at regular intervals thereafter, in line with state Medicaid standards. To conduct the assessments, some states used specially selected, trained, or dedicated personnel to increase the likelihood that the children received appropriate health care services. Limited research associates the existence of specific assessment policies or use of specialized personnel with higher rates of screening and referral than occur when policies are not specific or personnel have no specific training. Similarly, some state officials indicated that such assessment policies, including the use of designated providers, have allowed them to provide follow-up treatment more quickly than before these practices were in place.

To ensure the delivery of appropriate health services, most states we studied reported adopting one or more practices to facilitate access to services, coordinate health care, and review medications for children in foster care. These practices were intended to ensure that children's health services were not only delivered in a timely way, but in a consistent and complementary way across each step of the health care delivery process. In one case, a state used specialized staff to ensure that children in foster care were quickly reviewed for Medicaid eligibility. Other efforts included increasing payment rates to physicians for children in foster care to encourage more physicians to provide needed care. With regard to coordination of care, state practices included using nurses or other health care managers to help ensure that children in foster care received necessary health care services. In addition, several of the selected states identified practices related to monitoring the use of psychotropic medications—drugs commonly used for the treatment of mental health disorders—owing to their effects on thought, behavior, or mood. For example, one state requires a review of prescriptions in certain circumstances, such as when multiple psychotropic medications are prescribed at the same time. Officials in this state reported that after the policy took effect, there was a decrease in the number of children in foster care who were prescribed multiple psychotropic medications.

To document and monitor children's health care, some states we studied reported having data management practices that included sharing health care data across programs, and three states and a major city within another state pointed to various quality assurance mechanisms to track receipt of services. Data sharing with Medicaid and other data sources has helped some states we studied develop and maintain health records. In one state, these data sharing efforts include a foster care health "passport" that electronically compiles data on a specific child from multiple data systems, such as immunization records and data on prescription medications. This system allows for continuous updating at many points of care and permits access by multiple parties with decision-making responsibility for the child's health. Most state child welfare agencies we contacted reported using a combination of electronic and paper-based data sharing to obtain information other state agencies have compiled on children prior to their entry into foster care to provide more complete and timely medical histories than are otherwise available. However, these states provided more limited access to these data, and updates typically relied on the exchange of paper reports about medical visits and their results among doctors, foster parents, and caseworkers. In addition, the three states we visited and one major city reported having quality assurance activities that could be used to help monitor the receipt of services for children in foster care. For example, officials of some states we studied cited specialized case reviews focusing on children's receipt of health care services as supports in monitoring performance in meeting the health needs of children in their care.

ACF supports a network of 25 technical assistance centers to help state child welfare agencies improve their capacity to meet children's needs, including their health care needs. ACF officials explain that they do not expect the centers to provide technical assistance regarding medical services, but instead to help child welfare agencies carry out their broader mission to ensure the safety, wellbeing, and attainment of permanent homes for children in their care. With respect to the health of children in foster care, ACF officials stated that this may involve helping child welfare agencies work collaboratively with other agencies that provide health care services, including other federally and nonfederally funded public and nonprofit programs. One of ACF's 25 centers focuses exclusively on children's mental health, and several other centers have also assisted in identifying some practices designed to improve the health of children in foster care. Included among ACF's centers are five new centers that are due to become operational in 2009 and are expected to provide in-depth, long-term assistance in implementing plans to improve agency performance in meeting children's needs.

We provided a draft of this chapter to HHS for its comment. The agency provided some additional information on its technical assistance to state foster care agencies, particularly through collaboration between ACF and SAMHSA in efforts to assist states to address health issues such as mental health and substance abuse that may affect children in foster care. HHS's comments are reprinted in appendix II. HHS also provided technical comments, which we considered and incorporated as appropriate.

BACKGROUND

Children in foster care tend to exhibit more numerous and serious medical conditions than other children, including mental health problems. Foster care begins when children are removed from their parents or guardians and placed under the responsibility of a state child welfare agency. Removal from the home can occur for several reasons. For example, parental violence, substance abuse, severe depression, or incarceration may have led to the children's removal from the home. Other children and youth are referred when their own behaviors or conditions are beyond the control of their families or pose a threat to themselves or the community.

The realities of foster care may further contribute to the challenges in meeting these children's health care needs. Once children are removed from their homes, obtaining information on their health status and health history from their parents or guardians may be challenging. Also, children often move to several different foster homes or treatment facilities during the course of their stay in foster care, which may result in having different health care providers. Changes in placement pose significant challenges for agencies, foster parents, and providers with regard to providing continuity of health care services and maintaining uninterrupted information on children's medical needs and course of treatment.

Finally, in addition to specific characteristics or circumstances that complicate their care, children in foster care encounter some health care challenges in common with other health care users. Child welfare agencies generally expect that foster parents or other caregivers will recognize when children need medical attention and obtain the needed health services, but such services may be in short supply or difficult to access because of a lack of providers who serve Medicaid patients—particularly for some specialties or geographic areas. Children entering foster care may lack medical care prior to entry, and children with prior medical care may have experienced disruptions in care, changes in providers, and have missing or incomplete records.

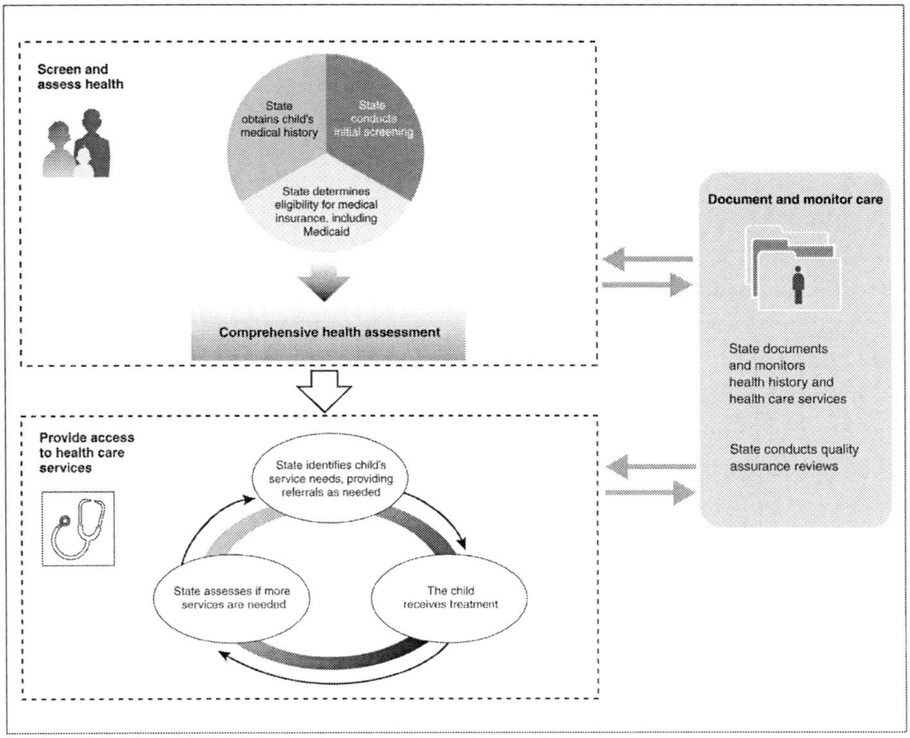

Sources: GAO analysis; images, Art Explosion (clip art).

Figure 1. Steps Typically Involved in Addressing Health Needs of Children in Foster Care

Figure 1 illustrates the steps that are typically involved in addressing health needs of children in foster care.[6]

State and Federal Funding for Children in Foster Care

All state child welfare agencies receive federal funds from ACF for children in foster care under two parts of title IV of the Social Security Act. The larger source of federal funds, under title IV-E, provides open-ended reimbursement for a portion of states' foster care expenses for children meeting federal eligibility criteria, who represented about 43 percent of children in foster care in 2006.[7] Title IV-E provided $4.8 billion to states in 2007 for the federal share of the expense of housing and feeding these children.[8] States cover the remaining costs and 100 percent of the costs to house and feed children in foster care who do not meet federal eligibility criteria. State child welfare agencies also receive funds under title IV-B to provide services to children in foster care and to those remaining in their homes for the purpose of preventing conditions leading to the need to remove children from their homes.[9] In 2007, about $700 million was available under title IV-B. State child welfare agencies cannot use title IV-E or most IV-B funds for the direct provision of health care services. Limited IV-B funds may be used for some health care services but are intended primarily for the support and preservation of families, rather than for children in foster care.[10] Foster children who meet title IV-E eligibility criteria, on the other hand, are explicitly identified as a group that is eligible for coverage under Medicaid.

As a condition of receiving federal funds, state child welfare agencies must agree to meet certain federal requirements, including requirements related to the health of children in foster care. Under both titles IV-B and IV-E, states must submit plans to ACF that contain a number of statutorily required elements. For title IV-E, state agencies must have a written case plan for each child that includes specific health information, such as records of immunizations and medications, to be shared with foster care providers at the time of placement. The agencies must also have standards to ensure that children are provided services to protect their safety and health. Because these standards have not been further defined in statute or regulation, states have some flexibility with respect to their form and content. For safety and health standards, some states have cited standards for licensing foster care facilities, training foster care parents, or credentialing staff.

In recent years, Congress has twice amended title IV-B, subpart 1 to add new state plan requirements related to the health of children served by child welfare agencies. Congress initially required that state plans describe the involvement of physicians and other medical professionals in the assessment and treatment of children in foster care.[11] This requirement was effective with state plans approved by ACF in 2007. In October 2008, as we completed our review, Congress further amended title IV-B, subpart 1 to require state agencies to develop plans for the ongoing oversight and coordination of health care services for children in foster care.[12] This new requirement expanded on the earlier requirement by mandating that the agencies include in their plans schedules for initial and follow-up health screenings that meet reasonable standards of medical practice; steps to ensure continuity of health care services, which may include the establishment of a medical home—a primary health care provider or group—for every child in care; oversight of prescription medications; and information on how children's needs identified through screenings will be monitored and treated and how their medical information will be updated and appropriately shared—as for example, by using electronic health records. These requirements apply to all children in foster care, regardless of whether or not the children meet federal eligibility criteria.

Federal Oversight and Technical Assistance

Starting in 2001, ACF took a new, results-oriented approach to its oversight of state child welfare programs, focusing on whether children and their families served by these programs achieved positive outcomes. This oversight effort involved four phases of Child and Family Services Reviews (CFSR), as shown in figure 2. ACF expects to complete the final phase of the initial round of CFSRs in 2009.

In the second phase of the initial round of the reviews completed in 2004, ACF identified significant performance challenges, particularly with respect to meeting children's mental health needs.[13] ACF assessed state child welfare agency performance on 45 indicators across a wide range of areas, such as children's safety and statewide information systems. On the two health indicators addressing physical and mental health, ACF identified 20 states as showing strengths in providing services to meet children's physical health needs, and 4 states also showed strengths in meeting the mental health needs of children in foster care and children remaining in their homes under agency supervision.[14] Nearly all states were required to implement program improvement plans because they did not show strengths in physical health, mental health, or both. ACF is required by statute to offer technical assistance, to the extent feasible, to help such states develop and implement plans to improve outcomes for children, including health outcomes. When ACF determines that a state has not met the jointly developed goals and action steps identified in these plans within 2 years of approval of the improvement plan, ACF regulations specify that it will withhold a portion of the state's grant funds.[15] In the course of its oversight, ACF identified several challenges that states faced in meeting the health needs of children in their care, as summarized in table 1.

Table 1. Findings of ACF Reviews with Respect to Common Challenges States Faced in Meeting Children's Health Needs

Physical health	Mental health
Number of physicians and dentists in the state willing to accept Medicaid is not sufficient to meet the need.[a]	There is a lack of mental health services for children in the state.
The state agency is not consistent in conducting adequate, timely health assessments.	The state agency is not consistent in conducting mental health assessments.
The state agency is not consistent in providing children with preventive health or dental services.	

Source: ACF, Summary of the Results of the 2001 - 2004 Child and Family Services Reviews, p.10, http://www.acf.hhs.gov/ programs/cb/cwmonitoring/results/ index.htm (accessed on Nov. 21, 2008).

[a] See GAO, *Medicaid: Extent of Dental Disease in Children Has Not Decreased and Millions Are Estimated to Have Untreated Tooth Decay*, GAO-08-1121 (Washington, D.C.: Sept. 23, 2008).

Medicaid and Health Care Services for Children in Foster Care

Medicaid is the primary health care funding source for most children in foster care.[16] The Medicaid program is administered at the federal level by the HHS's Centers for Medicare & Medicaid Services (CMS) and is jointly financed by the states and the federal government. All state Medicaid agencies receive federal funds for the Medicaid program under title XIX of the Social Security Act. Within broad parameters set by federal statute and regulation, state Medicaid agencies are responsible for determining eligibility and establishing the services and payments offered. Although many coverage, eligibility, and administrative decisions are left to individual states, the federal government sets certain requirements for state Medicaid programs, such as coverage of certain screening and treatment services.

Children who meet federal eligibility criteria for IV-E foster care are required to be covered by state Medicaid programs under federal law.[17] In addition, states have chosen to extend Medicaid coverage to other children in foster care.[18] In 2004, Medicaid expenditures for children in foster care exceeded $5 billion.[19]

Children in foster care who are enrolled in Medicaid may receive services through one of two distinct service delivery and financing systems—managed care and fee-for-service. Under a capitated managed care model, states contract with a managed care organization and prospectively pay the plans a fixed monthly fee per patient to provide or arrange for most health services. Plans, in turn, pay providers. In the traditional fee-for-service delivery system, the Medicaid program reimburses providers directly and on a retrospective basis for each service delivered.[20]

States are required to offer certain screening and treatment services to children enrolled in Medicaid.[21] Termed Early and Periodic Screening, Diagnostic, and Treatment services (EPSDT), these screenings must include, but are not limited to, a comprehensive health and developmental history, a comprehensive unclothed physical exam, appropriate immunizations, laboratory tests, and health education. The required services include vision, dental, hearing, and services for other conditions discovered through screenings, regardless of whether these services are typically covered by the state's Medicaid program for other beneficiaries. The state Medicaid agencies establish standards for the timing and frequency of these screening and treatment services and set their own payment rates for fee-for-service providers of these services. Federal regulations require that EPSDT screening services be provided in accordance with reasonable standards of medical and dental practice determined by the state after consultation with recognized medical and dental organizations involved in child health care.[22]

In addition to EPSDT, states may choose to offer optional Medicaid benefits, such as rehabilitative services and targeted case management for children in foster care. States have used the rehabilitative services option for children in foster care who have mental or developmental problems as a means of providing a wide range of services designed to help them achieve their highest level of functioning. States have used targeted case management in order to provide case management services to a defined group of Medicaid-eligible individuals, such as children in foster care.[23] Such case management activities have included assessing a child's needs, developing plans to meet those needs, referring a child to services, monitoring the receipt of such services, and ensuring any necessary follow-up care.

Federal Medicaid funds are available for a portion of case management activities, as long as funds are not available from other programs or from other

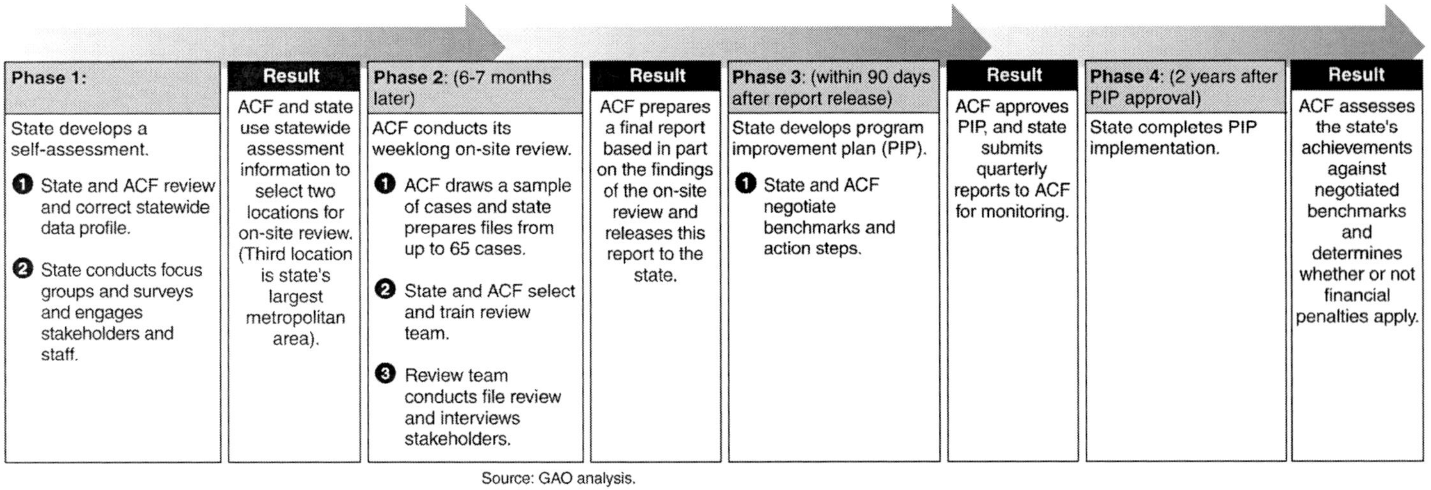

Source: GAO analysis.

Figure 2. Four Phases of the Initial Round of the CFSR Process

entities, such as other insurers, that would be legally obligated to pay for such services.[24] However, concerns exist that Medicaid funds have been inappropriately used,[25] and CMS has denied payment for services when funds were available from other programs, such as Title IV-E.26 In 2007, CMS issued rules—an interim final rule for case management services and a proposed rule on Medicaid program coverage for rehabilitative services—that further defined the use of Medicaid funds for these benefits for children in foster care.[27] However, in 2008, Congress passed and the President signed into law a moratorium on certain aspects of the rules that remains in effect until April 1, 2009.[28]

Other HHS Agencies

In addition to ACF and CMS, other agencies within HHS have roles in sustaining the health of foster children through supporting research, providing grants, or offering technical assistance that may assist with providing necessary health care services to children in foster care, as shown below:

- The Agency for Healthcare Research and Quality is responsible for supporting research designed to improve the quality of healthcare, reduce its costs, address patient safety and medical errors, and broaden access to essential services;
- the Health Resources and Services Administration (HRSA) administers programs related to maternal and child health, as well as services specific to particular conditions, such as human immunodeficiency virus and acquired immune deficiency syndrome (HIV and AIDS); and
- SAMHSA funds programs and services for individuals—as well as their families and communities—who suffer from or are at risk for substance abuse or mental health disorders.

Specific Requirements for Health Assessments—and Using Designated Providers to Conduct Them—Are Employed to Identify Children's Health Care Needs

To help facilitate the timely identification of foster children's health care needs, all 10 states we examined had adopted specific policies with regard to the timing and scope of assessments, and 4 of these states also reported using designated providers to conduct the assessments. The policies generally call for assessments shortly after children enter care and take one of two forms: (1) a two-stage assessment comprised of an initial screening followed by a comprehensive assessment or (2) a single comprehensive assessment. Most states we selected for study included a requirement for screening of children's mental health and developmental needs, and most of the states we studied cited substance abuse screenings. Researchers and state officials have suggested that having designated providers conduct assessments may improve the quality and utility of assessment results. State officials report that these assessment practices have allowed them to make more appropriate and lasting placements of children in foster care and also to provide follow-up treatment more quickly than before these practices were in place. Some research also links specific assessment policies to higher rates of follow-up.

Specific Requirements Can Ensure Timely, Appropriate Initial and Comprehensive Assessments

While federal law did not specifically require assessments before fiscal year 2009, the 10 states we reviewed had made assessments of children's physical health mandatory for all children entering care, as recommended by medical and other professional associations.[29] Because children often enter foster care with serious health conditions and, at times, without easily accessible medical histories, it is important to identify their health needs as quickly as possible. Health or developmental status may be a critical factor in determining the appropriate placement and level of care for children, as in the case of children with HIV or significant behavioral problems. Where there are explicit and comprehensive policies mandating assessments of all children entering care, greater percentages of children are likely to be assessed, according to a survey of a nationally representative sample of child welfare agencies.[30] Further analysis of these survey data showed that agencies with comprehensive developmental screening policies were more likely to evaluate children, refer them to early intervention agencies, and engage in joint planning of health care services.[31]

Officials from the 10 states we reviewed reported using two general approaches to conducting assessments, but all required some health assessment within 30 days of a child's removal from his or her home. Florida, Illinois, Massachusetts, and New York generally conduct screenings or assessments in two stages: (1) an initial screening within 24 hours to 7 days to check for immediate health needs and (2) a later, fuller assessment within 30 days of entry into foster care.[32] Some state officials expressed the view that waiting a while for the fuller assessment may give children the opportunity to adjust to their changed circumstances and for this reason may offer providers a more accurate picture of the children's health. Additionally, they noted that assessments may be lengthy and require significant time to complete. For example, Florida officials explained that their comprehensive assessment of mental health, development, and substance abuse takes 20 hours to complete, double the amount of time the state previously allotted in order to cover all necessary aspects of care. A second approach to identifying children's health care needs—used by California, Delaware, Oklahoma, Texas, Utah and Washington—invokes a one-stage assessment process mandating that it be completed within 14 to 30 days of entry into foster care depending on the state.[33] Utah officials explained that the state dropped its earlier requirement for an initial screening followed by another assessment, in part because the results were duplicative. However, the state expects caseworkers to be alert to urgent health needs and arrange treatment as needed. The state has written guidelines advising caseworkers that if there is any sign of abuse or neglect or if the child is ill, the child should be seen by a health care provider within 24 hours.

Once a child enters foster care and receives an initial assessment, state foster care policies in most of the states we selected for study required that ongoing assessments follow the schedules established by state Medicaid agencies for children's screening, which are based on the children's age or the time between routine checkups.[34] Six of the 10 states we selected for our study called for children in foster care to receive at least annual screening, either under a separate health standard applicable to foster children or because their EPSDT standard for all Medicaid enrollees called for at least annual screenings, consistent with the 2008 American Academy of Pediatrics' recommendation on preventive pediatric care. See table 2 for a summary of the number of EPSDT screens incorporated in the Medicaid EPSDT standard for all children in the Medicaid programs in the 10 states we reviewed.

In addition to policies requiring assessments of children's physical health, 8 of the 10 states we studied also reported requiring screening or assessments of children's mental and developmental health shortly after entry into foster care. Research indicates that an estimated 30 to 60 percent of children in foster care may have chronic health conditions, and the proportion estimated to have serious health care needs rises to over 80 percent when behavioral, emotional, and developmental concerns are included.[35] Guidelines issued by professional

Table 2. Number of EPSDT Screens for Medicaid-Enrolled Children in Selected Age Groups, by State[a]

		Age group			
State	**Less than 1**	**1-5**	**6-14**	**15-20**	**Total**
California[b]	6	6	3	1	**15**
Delaware	7	8	9	6	**30**
Florida[c]	7	7	7[d]	6	**27**
Illinois[d]	7	7	5	3	**22**
Massachusetts	6	7	9	6	**28**
New York	7	8	9	6	**30**
Oklahoma	5	7	4	4	**20**
Texas	5	7	7	6	**25**
Utah	6	7	7	6	**26**
Washington[e]	5	6	5	3	**19**

Source: GAO analysis of states' EPSDT screening requirements.

[a] Because some states used age categories in describing their policies that did not align with those shown here, the distribution of screens across age groups is an approximation, with no screen counted more than once.

[b] California adopted a screening schedule based on an earlier American Academy of Pediatrics screening schedule. According to state officials, California is in the process of updating the state's screening schedule to conform to the most recent American Academy of Pediatrics screening schedule.

[c] Florida follows the 1999 American Academy of Pediatrics schedule, which recommended a total of 27 screens. Florida Medicaid also recommends check-ups at 7 and 9 years of age for "children at risk."

[d] Illinois recommends that health screening be provided to children on a periodicity schedule based on acceptable medical practice standards, such as the schedule recommended by the American Academy of Pediatrics. The schedule above was provided by the Illinois Department of Public Aid, now known as the Illinois Department of Healthcare and Family Services, as a minimum guideline for children in the Medicaid program. The Illinois Department of Children and Family Services requires that children in foster care receive at minimum annual health screenings between the ages of 6 and 21.

[e] The Washington EPSDT standard specifies annual screening for children in foster care between the ages of 2 and 20.

associations emphasize the importance of assessing mental health and other behavioral health issues for children in foster care. An analysis of the results of ACF reviews conducted between 2001 and 2004 found no evidence of policies requiring an assessment of children's mental health in most states; in one state, stakeholders noted that children did not get mental health assessments unless there were problems observed.[36] The ACF reviews have helped focus attention on the mental health needs of children in foster care, however, and we found that most of the 10 states we selected for study had adopted policies to screen or assess the mental health and development of children entering foster care. Most states we studied had also adopted policies requiring or recommending screening youth entering foster care for substance abuse. For example, Delaware officials told us that—since February 2006—its initial health screening has required the inclusion of a component alerting staff to any mental health or substance abuse problems for all children 4 through 17 years of age. Other state policies varied in whether or not they included specific time frames. For example, New York has no mandatory time frame for its required mental health assessment, although it is recommended that this be completed within 30 days of placement. State guidance also varies on the tools used for the assessments. In some states, such as Massachusetts, the steps taken by individual health practitioners as part of either (1) the comprehensive screening within the first 30 days or (2) in later Medicaid screenings are considered sufficient to meet the policy requirements. In other cases, states have adopted or are considering adopting specific screening tools. For example, Utah reported the state had specified the tools to be used in assessing the development of children ages 4 months to 5 years. Officials in both California and Oklahoma reported they were working to identify assessment instruments for the early identification of children with mental health or developmental needs.

The Use of Designated Providers Can Increase the Thoroughness of Physical and Mental Health Assessments

Four states we studied reported using designated providers to perform certain initial and comprehensive assessments, which some evidence indicates can increase the consistency and thoroughness with which children's physical and mental health needs are identified. Illinois, for example, requires that children's initial health evaluations be conducted by a network of hospital emergency rooms and clinics, while subsequent assessments are generally conducted by a network of community- and facility-based physicians, with foster parents permitted to use others on request. We identified two studies that associated use of designated or specialized health care providers for foster children with higher rates of preventive and specialty care.[37]

Table 3. Examples of States' Approaches to Using Designated Providers for Physical Health Assessments

State	Description of approach
Florida	• Some counties within Florida use a network of physicians to conduct initial screenings for children in foster care.
	• Such networks may serve as a medical home for children throughout and beyond their stay in foster care.
Illinois	• Illinois has a network of providers who conduct initial health screenings, comprehensive health evaluations, and ongoing primary care for all children in foster care, and some comprehensive evaluation providers may serve as sources of continuing care.
	• Providers may be located in hospitals or clinics, with hospital emergency rooms or clinics serving as the initial screening location for children.
Oklahoma	• Oklahoma uses primary care providers in clinics in Oklahoma City and Tulsa to screen children for physical, mental health, and dental needs, as well as any social needs.
	• The clinic location can serve as a medical home for the child after assessment.
Utah	• Children entering custody with a medical home are to be sent to their original provider for the comprehensive health assessment.
	• For children in foster care who do not have an identified medical home, Utah uses providers located in a public health clinic in Salt Lake City to provide initial screening and comprehensive health assessments to local children in foster care.
	• The clinic can serve as a medical home for the child after assessment.

Source: GAO analysis of state interview responses, as of August 2008.

With regard to physical assessments, states that identified the use of designated providers to perform initial screens and comprehensive assessments reported that these providers functioned as part of a network of providers, as primary providers in specific locations, or both and, in some cases, that the use of such networks had enhanced the numbers receiving assessments. For example, Florida reported that some of its counties have focused on developing a network of trained providers, while Oklahoma and Utah identified specific locations in urban areas—such as clinics or hospitals—where some children could receive assessments. In most cases, these initial providers could serve as medical homes for the children they assessed. (See table 3 for more information on how states use designated providers.) Some state officials commented that the use of a specific network of physicians also facilitated quality improvement efforts. For example, a physician with Cook County's Healthworks program noted that the quality of health assessments—once a subject of complaint from child welfare field staff—had improved when assessments were channeled to a network of specific providers that could be supported by targeted training efforts. He noted that the health assessment for a child entering foster care requires a more thorough, detailed approach and level of documentation than that involved in a standard EPSDT well-child exam.

The states shown in the table as using designated providers elaborated on their practices and, in some instances, noted specific strategies that may contribute to providers' effectiveness:

- Illinois requires that the initial health screening be completed within an hour of the child's arrival at the medical facility. Illinois officials reported that appointments for the screening in Cook County are arranged through a toll-free telephone service called HealthLine, which is staffed around the clock by a child welfare contractor who can obtain priority service for children so they do not experience lengthy waits in hospital emergency rooms. Hospital emergency rooms are used for many initial screenings because they are accessible outside of normal business hours, but the comprehensive health assessments generally take place in physicians' offices because they require more time. Research on children enrolled in the Illinois program has shown that these children experienced higher rates of preventive and necessary specialty care than other children with similar socio-economic characteristics who were not enrolled in the program. Although the research did not evaluate the effectiveness of the program itself, the researchers concluded that the increased attention and oversight of the health care for the children enrolled in the program affected their outcomes.[38]
- Oklahoma officials noted that their clinic-based assessment process began with a pediatrician who had experience working with children who had been removed from their homes and placed into shelters. Concerned about the continuity of care for children in these situations, this pediatrician set aside particular times for children in foster care to visit the clinic and see a familiar provider. A second clinic that was opened in another large city is also under the medical direction of a pediatrician

familiar with the needs of children in foster care. Officials told us they believe that children's health care benefits when they are served by providers with knowledge of the foster care population.

In addition to using designated providers for physical health screens and comprehensive assessments, a few states reported using a mental health specialist who worked with caseworkers to conduct assessments. The use of specialists to conduct mental health screenings can be an effective means of identifying children's mental health needs. One study that surveyed a nationally representative sample of agencies found that involving mental health specialists in assessments resulted in a greater identification of mental health needs, as well as improved follow-up care, than were received by children whose assessments did not include a mental health specialist.[39]

The mental health assessments used by states we selected varied. In some cases, the assessments were comprehensive social assessments that covered areas such as mental health, emotional health, school, work, and community involvement. In other cases, the focus was narrower, covering specific topics such as indicators of mental illness. Washington officials reported that specialized social workers conducted comprehensive assessments using standardized tools that assess several aspects of social and mental health needs, including behavioral, developmental, educational, family, and social issues.[40] For physical or mental health concerns identified during the screening that require treatment, state officials indicated that the social workers refer children to appropriate health care professionals.

PRACTICES TO ENHANCE ACCESS TO SERVICES, COORDINATE CARE, AND MONITOR USE OF MEDICATIONS ARE AMONG EFFORTS TO ENSURE DELIVERY OF HEALTH CARE TO FOSTER CHILDREN

To address the challenge of ensuring delivery of appropriate health care services to children in foster care, several of the states we selected for review adopted practices designed to facilitate access to care, coordinate services, and review medications for children in foster care. Practices relating to access to care included efforts to hasten determination of Medicaid eligibility, implement financial incentives for providers to serve children in foster care, and enhance access to medical specialists for various subgroups of children. Care coordination practices that the selected states identified employed either nurses or other health care managers to help ensure that children in foster care received necessary health care services. Officials of specific states we contacted said that such care coordination had increased rates of immunization, initial assessment, and well-child visits. Finally, officials from six of the states we studied pointed to policies that they had implemented requiring the review of prescriptions for psychotropic medications commonly used to treat mental health disorders for children in foster care.

Practices to Enhance Access to Care Include Streamlined Medicaid Eligibility, Financial Incentives to Providers, and Strategies to Obtain Specialty Care

Among the states we studied that identified a practice state officials believed noteworthy in enhancing access to care, some had identified assigning certain staff—from their Medicaid offices or from their child welfare offices—to ensure that children in foster care were quickly reviewed for Medicaid eligibility. Because the removal of a child from home can change his or her Medicaid eligibility status, some states we contacted had taken steps to save time in certifying Medicaid eligibility and facilitate new foster care beneficiaries' access to providers. For example, Delaware had assigned two Medicaid staff to foster care cases, while Florida, Utah, and Illinois used staff members from the child welfare offices to determine eligibility for Medicaid. Utah has a written agreement between the state child welfare and Medicaid agencies that specifies that certain staff in Utah's Division of Child and Family Services will determine Medicaid eligibility for children in foster care. The purpose of this arrangement is to enhance services to children and families, simplify administration, improve accuracy, conserve state resources by avoiding duplication, and maximize legitimate Medicaid funding. In Illinois, children coming into foster care are presumed to be eligible for Medicaid. For purposes of formal eligibility determination, Illinois officials reported that using specialized staff members in the state child welfare agency's central office to complete the determination had sped up the process. Specifically, they reported that a process that once took 3 to 4 months could now be completed within 4 weeks of issuance of the temporary medical card. Florida officials also reported that their agreement that staff from the child welfare department determine Medicaid eligibility reduced the amount of time required to make these determinations from 18 days to within 24 hours.

Illinois and Washington are among the states that offer financial incentives to providers who treat children in foster care, since providers may be reluctant to serve children in foster care. In Illinois, physicians serving children in foster care are paid a one-time $15 fee to initiate a paper health passport to document the health history and ongoing care of the child. Additionally, the state uses an enhanced payment rate for initial health screenings conducted in hospital emergency rooms.[41] Washington officials reported that the state increased its payments in November 2001 for medical providers who conducted well-child examinations for children in foster care. At the time, these rates were about twice the reimbursement rate paid in other cases. State officials reported that since 2001, other Medicaid rates—such as payments for EPSDT services—have also increased, so that rates for foster care children are no longer twice as high. However, the foster care rates remain equal to or substantially greater than the standard Medicaid rates. In April 2008, Washington officials told us that approximately two-thirds of children received well-child examinations, up from about 17 percent before the state increased the rates in 2001.

Utah, Illinois, and New York have instituted a variety of programs to increase access to medical specialists or subspecialists. Under some circumstances, obtaining specialty care can be difficult for Medicaid-eligible children, and such efforts for children in foster care may be even more difficult if the children have complex health needs or changing placements. These states' efforts typically focused on specific subgroups of children in foster care, such as those in rural areas, those who need mental health services, and those who would otherwise require institutional care.

- *Children in Rural Areas*: Utah and Illinois have efforts focused on children living in rural areas where it may be harder to find a pediatric health specialist or subspecialist. For example, Utah has eight clinics to which multidisciplinary teams travel in order to provide specialty services for children with special health care needs across rural Utah. State officials told us that in some cases, children are seen more quickly in these locations than in Salt Lake City. Illinois officials reported transportation is available and sometimes is used to get rural foster children to providers, including oral dental surgeons, orthodontists, and child psychiatrists. Despite these efforts, state child welfare officials cited a continuing challenge in obtaining mental health and substance abuse services, and especially child psychiatry for children in Medicaid and other publicly-funded medical care, not just those in foster care. As a result, Illinois has also begun to look at the use of telepsychiatry in one of its downstate regions.[42]

- *Children Needing Mental Health Services*: To address children who are experiencing mental health crises, Illinois developed a psychiatric crisis intervention program with a single, statewide 24-hour, 7-day-a-week crisis hotline. When a person calls the crisis line, a mental health provider is expected to reach the child in crisis within 90 minutes of the call to conduct a screening and determine if the child requires psychiatric hospitalization. Following this decision, the mental health provider is to continue to provide treatment and other service interventions for a minimum of 90 days. State officials reported that this program serves about 18,000 children per year, including all children who receive Medicaid or other public funding for medical care (not just those in foster care). Medicaid covers all the services provided by this program, which began in 2004, on a fee-for-service basis.
- *Children Who Might Otherwise Require Institutional Care*: With respect to difficulty in accessing specialty services, New York launched a program in early 2008 for children in foster care who have developmental disabilities, serious emotional disturbances, and medical problems that are so severe they would otherwise likely be in restrictive and high-cost institutions. By making community-based services available to a fixed number of these children, the state hopes to help them function in family and community settings instead. New York officials reported that when the program is fully implemented after 2011, it will serve approximately 3,000 children in foster care.

Public Health Nurses and Other Health Care Managers Coordinate Care to Help Ensure Health Services Are Delivered Appropriately

Several states we studied discussed their development of the role of health care managers with the goal of improving health care and health outcomes for children in foster care. While all children in foster care have caseworkers, they focus on issues related to the child's safety and permanency and do not necessarily have medical expertise. Typically, health care managers are nurses who are colocated with the child welfare agency and work with the child's foster care caseworker. Officials in California told us that the nurses are colocated in the child welfare offices so they can easily talk directly to caseworkers. These nurses may be able to more quickly spot gaps in care than foster care caseworkers because they are trained to understand children's health and developmental needs, they are able to communicate clearly with health care providers, and they can provide medical guidance to both foster care caseworkers and foster and biological parents. In some states—such as California and Utah—each child is assigned a nurse, while in other states—such as Illinois and Massachusetts—only those children with specific or medically complex needs are individually assigned to a nurse. In some states, public health nurses provided the care coordination services for children in foster care, whereas in Illinois, the state child welfare agency or a local contracting agency served as health care manager. Some positive results in achieving health-related goals for children in foster care had been documented for a health care management effort in New York.[43]

The specific services provided by health care managers varied in the states we contacted, but usually included the development and maintenance of the child's health history, medical case planning—that is, identifying the child's medical needs and arranging for receipt of medical services—and identification of medical professionals available to provide services to children in foster care. For example, state officials in Utah told us that the state has 29 Maternal and Child Health agency nurses serving about 90 children each. The nurses may provide medical, mental health, and dental consultation; identify the child's primary care provider; place the child in the appropriate health plan; gather, evaluate, and document the health history of each child; track ongoing health care; and maintain an up-to-date medical history on each child within an electronic database.[44] Officials in Utah reported that use of public health nurses has reduced errors in transcribing information about medical history and ongoing care into the state's electronic database. Utah officials also reported that they find that biological parents are more comfortable talking openly with the nurse, who they said biological parents tend to view as an advocate rather than an adversary. According to data provided by state officials, another result of the program is that more children are getting their comprehensive assessments completed than before, and more quickly than required. Specifically, Utah officials reported that about 76 percent of children received these assessments in a timely fashion in 2008, compared to 58 percent in 1998, before the program was implemented. They further noted that these assessments are being conducted in 18 days, on average, rather than taking the full 30 days allowed by state requirements.

Health care managers may also provide other services. Caseworkers in Illinois told us that in medically complex situations, families can be assigned to a regional nurse who can provide recommendations and assist a caseworker in communicating with the family on medical needs. Similarly, in Massachusetts, staff told us that nurses in regional offices provide consultation to staff regarding the medical needs of all children and work with children who have difficult or complex medical needs. In Illinois, officials at one of the privately-run case management programs in Chicago became concerned about immunization and well-child exam completion rates. As a result, they implemented a paper-based reminder recall system that gives foster parents, providers, and caseworkers information about when and what medical services are needed. Prior to the implementation of the reminder-recall system, officials in one agency that had adopted it told us that 77 percent of children had up-to-date immunizations and 44 percent had received appropriate well-child visits. These officials reported that in 2007, after implementation of this reminder-recall system, 96 percent received appropriate immunizations and 90 percent had received well-child care. We were told that the five community-based medical care management agencies in Cook County used the reminder-recall system.[45] In addition, some counties outside of Cook County have instituted a similar system.

New York conducted a formal evaluation of its health care management project and found that such care coordination had a significant, positive impact on many aspects of care, including the receipt of both initial physical and dental assessments, access to nonpreventative care, and health-related contacts between agency workers and foster parents.[46] However, funding was not available for the state to continue this program when the initial pilot project was completed and the project did not meet nonhealth and well-being related child welfare goals, such as reducing the number of days spent in foster care and increasing the likelihood of leaving foster care for a permanent placement.

Policies Governing the Review of Psychotropic Medications Implemented to Help Ensure Children in Foster Care Receive Appropriate Health Care

Officials in six of the states we selected for interview identified specific policies they had adopted to govern the review of psychotropic medications intended for the treatment of mental health disorders.[47] An Illinois official noted that the use of psychotropic medications is uniquely challenging for children in foster care, given that foster children who change placements often do not have a consistent person to plan treatment, offer consent, and provide oversight. Most of the policies states identified require an extra level of review beyond the person prescribing the medication, either by state officials or local experts. Concerns have been expressed that psychotropic medications have frequently not been tested for their safety and efficacy with children, and one study of children in foster care found that the most frequently prescribed medication was an antipsychotic drug that had not been tested for use by children and adolescents.[48] Some research has also found that use of psychotropic drugs by children in foster care is three to four times greater than by other low-income children insured by Medicaid.[49] Greater prevalence of use is not, by itself, evidence of inappropriate use; children in foster care may be more likely to have conditions for which the drugs are indicated. However, administrative data from one state associated the introduction of its policy with modest decreases in prescribing psychotropic drugs and declines in specific patterns of prescribing, such as prescribing multiple drugs.

Texas has developed a policy that notes the importance of conducting a health history, psychosocial assessment, mental status exam, and physical exam before prescribing psychotropic medications. The policy suggests that alternative interventions should generally be considered before beginning the use of psychotropic medications and outlines specific circumstances under which a case may require further review.[50] Data examining the percentage of children prescribed a psychotropic medication for at least 60 days, the percentage prescribed two or more medications concurrently from the same drug class, and the percentage prescribed five or more medications concurrently showed decreases from fiscal year 2004, before the new policies were implemented, through fiscal year 2007.[51]

Because of concerns raised about the appropriate use of psychotropic medications, California requires judicial approval for their administration to a foster child. The prescribing physician must make the case to a juvenile court judge that the particular medication is appropriate for the given child and that alternatives have been considered. The Judicial Council of California has adopted rules of court to implement this legal requirement. Specifically, these rules require that an application be made to a juvenile court judge requesting the use of psychotropic medication and that the application include the signature of the physician to request the medication's use; the child's diagnosis, the specific medication, and dosage recommended for use; the anticipated benefits and possible side effects of the medication; a list of other medications the child is taking, along with a description of possible drug interactions; a description of other treatment plans; and a statement that the child has been informed of the recommended course of treatment with their responses. The court may grant the application or may delegate that authority to the parent if it is found that the parent poses no danger to the child and that the parent has the capacity to understand the request. In an emergency, the rules allow the administration of psychotropic medications without court approval in accordance with existing law, but court approval must be obtained within 2 days.

Other states have worked with universities and local experts to help with the oversight of psychotropic medication use by children in foster care. For example, Illinois has contracted with a university to provide an independent review of each psychotropic medication request to ensure safe and appropriate usage with children in foster care. The request is forwarded to a board-certified child and adolescent psychiatrist who reviews the information and determines whether to approve, deny, or adjust the request. According to state officials, Florida has also worked with a local university to develop a process whereby caregivers of children in foster care receive a consultation with a physician before psychotropic medications are prescribed. The state also has a mandatory preconsent consultation for all children age 5 and under in foster care. The state then tracks information about the medication, such as the prescribing physician, medication, dosage, number of refills, and its purpose. As a result, the state is able to determine the number of children receiving certain types of medication and can then identify areas where there might be concerns about inappropriate use. Oklahoma and New York also work with experts to review and provide training related to the use of psychotropic medications by children in foster care.

Mechanisms for Data Management and Quality Assurance Address Challenges to Documenting and Monitoring Children's Health Care

To address the challenges of documenting and monitoring children's health care, some states we studied shared health care data across various state systems to acquire more complete medical histories and used quality assurance mechanisms, such as medical audits or specialized case reviews, to track receipt of services. Efforts to share health care data generally focused on enhancing access to existing health information among parties responsible for the health of children in foster care while meeting requirements for data security and privacy protection. For example, through data sharing with Medicaid and other data sources, Texas has developed an electronic health record—known as the Foster Care Health Passport—that can be viewed by authorized individuals involved in the child's care through a secure Web site. More commonly, states we studied identified initiatives that also combined data from different sources but did not offer electronic access or provide for any updating at the point of care, relying on paper-based transfers of medical histories and providers' updates via the foster parents. Quality assurance activities have also made use of electronic systems as a means of monitoring the receipt of services for children in foster care. These efforts can be important to ensuring that individual children receive the appropriate level of services, avoiding duplication of services such as immunizations, and ensuring the receipt of needed services.

Data Sharing with Medicaid and Other Systems May Yield More Complete Medical Information

Some states share data with Medicaid and other state systems, such as immunization registries, in order to obtain more complete medical information than might otherwise be available as a child enters foster care. Basic health information should be included in a written case plan and provided to foster parents before children are placed with them. Obtaining information that is important to a child's health records can be a complex task, which may involve four or more separate systems (see figure 3). Additionally, information collected from parents and caregivers may also be of assistance in understanding the needs of a child.

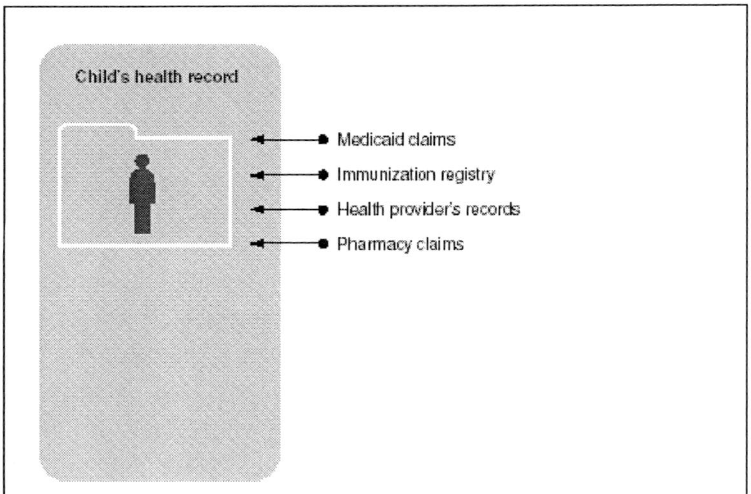

Source: GAO analysis; images, Art Explosion (clip art).

Figure 3. State Data Systems Used by One or More State Child Welfare Agencies to Develop the Health History of Children in Foster Care

States that pointed to records management systems as a means of developing health history cited the use of an electronic health record—sometimes termed an electronic passport—or other efforts to combine sources of information. Combining these sources of information is important because few children enter foster care with records that accurately identify their health providers, health conditions, or receipt of services. Without these records, their health care may be delayed until records are available, or their care may be compromised. For example, officials in two states told us of cases in which health providers had refused to provide specific treatments to children in foster care because they did not know their histories or did not have medical records available to prevent improper treatment. Similarly, children may miss immunizations, receive duplicate immunizations, or forego necessary medications.

Web-Based Electronic Passport Can Allow Access to Comprehensive Health Information on Individual Children in Foster Care

In April 2008, Texas began implementing an electronic passport to track health data for 29,000 children in foster care.[52] This passport can be updated regularly and is accessed through a secure Web site by foster parents, caseworkers, and health care providers who are responsible for making health decisions on behalf of children.[53] The Foster Care Health Passport is operated by a managed care organization that is under contract with the state Medicaid agency. Texas developed and implemented the Health Passport using funds from the state and CMS. Officials told us that total funding data were not readily available.

When a child enters the Texas foster care system, his or her electronic health record is created by obtaining information from a variety of sources. The Health Passport is initially populated with Medicaid and State Children's Health Insurance Program (SCHIP) claims, including pharmacy claims data from the past 2 years for children previously enrolled in Medicaid or SCHIP. Officials told us that generally, data from these sources are available for a majority, but not all, children who enter foster care. Immunization records are entered through a data sharing arrangement with the state's immunization registry. Once the electronic health record is created, it can be electronically updated with information on any health care services that were delivered by any foster care health provider in the managed care organization's network. Claims data are added when the claim is processed, which state officials indicated could take a few weeks or months, noting that providers have 90 days after a medical visit to submit a claim. Services provided outside of the contractor's network must be added manually through an online form mailed or faxed to the managed care organization. Officials told us that the passport also records behavioral health, dental, and vision services. Finally, officials stated that information in the Health Passport remains accessible statewide, even when the child's placement changes and the child moves to new foster parents, localities, or health providers. When children leave foster care, the electronic health record is printed out for the child or his caregiver.

While the Health Passport has not been operational long enough to determine its effectiveness, state officials told us that they are working on baseline measures for several variables, such as well-child outcomes, and have developed measures to assess the contractor's performance.[54]

Officials in several other states we contacted expressed an interest in pursuing the development of an electronic health passport. For example, Illinois uses several data systems to manage Medicaid, foster care, and community health and preventive care for children, but the state is working toward integrating data electronically from the many systems in use, with the ultimate goal being the construction of an electronic passport. Some obstacles to data sharing have included concerns about privacy and security. As states look to sharing individuals' health data to better serve and treat them, they are also implementing standards governing the transmission of data, policies to ensure that only authorized users have access to records, and provisions to protect individuals' privacy. CMS has taken steps to provide assistance to states on issues of security and privacy. Several of the states included in this study cited practices they used to create medical histories and agreements they have to address data security and privacy issues.

Other Forms of Data Sharing Can Improve Access to Timely Health Information

Other forms of data sharing use and combine existing record-keeping systems, usually through a combination of electronic matches and paper exchange of data among doctors, foster parents, and the Medicaid or the foster care agency, as shown in the examples below.

- Oklahoma officials noted that the state's efforts to obtain medical information for children entering foster care centered on using Medicaid claims data, which it has been doing on a statewide basis since 2007. State officials reported that the project has been particularly successful because over 90 percent of children entering foster care had some prior Medicaid history and over 80 percent were already on Medicaid when they entered the state's care. Officials noted that the Medicaid claims data can provide information on developmental assessments, immunizations, as well as the receipt of both physical and mental health services.

- In Utah and Illinois, nurses enter children's health information into the state child welfare agency's database. In Utah, public health nurses who work in collaboration with child welfare workers provide medical care coordination and record visits, diagnoses, and prescriptions for children in foster care. The child welfare agency in Illinois has a memorandum of agreement with its Medicaid agency to share pharmacy claims data for purposes of identifying doctors prescribing psychotropic medications without consent, and it also electronically obtains immunization data on children in foster care from an immunization registry. Both Utah and Illinois state officials told us that they were in the process of creating an integrated system that will store more complete electronic health records for children in foster care. For example, Illinois child welfare officials reported they were working with other state agencies to be able to pull data from Medicaid claims and other sources.
- Massachusetts uses a combination of paper and electronic records. They exchange medical information with foster parents and health care providers on paper, which they then enter into an electronic database.
- An official with HHS's Agency for Healthcare Research and Quality told us that health information exchanges in Colorado and Indiana are being developed with federal demonstration grants that will include foster children along with other patients. The HHS Inspector General reported in August 2007 that at least 27 states are developing at least partially electronic health records for Medicaid with funds from CMS. These efforts may extend to children in foster care but are not focused on them.[55]

Quality Assurance Activities Can Help Monitor the Receipt of Services

New York, Utah, Delaware, and Illinois specifically pointed to quality assurance activities relevant to monitoring foster children's receipt of health care services. Such activities can be used to help track the receipt of services by individual children in foster care, including ensuring that individual children are assessed as required and treated appropriately. Monitoring procedures that aggregate information across foster children can help managers ensure that health policies are consistently implemented and having the intended results.

The four states that discussed their quality assurance activities cited practices that included the use of technology and electronic records to collect, analyze, and aggregate health care data, perform medical audits, and conduct evaluations or other checks to ensure the quality of health care services provided to children in foster care. ACF's reviews found that states with identifiable quality assurance systems that conformed to specific criteria had a higher percentage of cases rated as having met the health needs of children in the states' custody. Further, ACF's analysis suggested that states with well-functioning quality assurance systems were more likely to succeed on measures of enhancing a family's capacity to provide for the needs of their children and ensuring that the children's physical and mental health needs were being met.[56]

The states that identified relevant quality assurance activities to us provided examples of two approaches: (1) requiring managed care organizations to track and report individual or aggregate data on foster children in their care and (2) conducting medical audits of health records for children in foster care.

With regard to requiring managed care organizations to track and report certain data, officials in Delaware described a new requirement in its contracts with managed care organizations aimed at ensuring that initial health screenings occur and result in the receipt of necessary services. In 2008, Delaware required that contracts with managed care organizations track and report on services rendered following initial health screenings. According to Delaware Medicaid officials, the reports are intended to provide aggregate data on health screenings provided. The officials told us that no specific concern triggered the 2008 quality check on initial health screenings, but officials noted that the state would like to be able to provide aggregate data on the percentage of children in their foster care program who received an initial health assessment within a set number of days. Utah uses a statewide case management system that can generate detailed data on individual children, as well as aggregate reports. Utah officials explained that these aggregate reports had been used to contact medical providers when the state received alerts from the U.S. Food and Drug Administration on the adverse effects of certain drugs. In this instance, the state sent letters to medical providers urging them to examine specific patients on these medications. Utah officials believed that having a majority of records in electronic form facilitated this effort.

Finally, one city and two states reported the use of medical audits to ensure the receipt and quality of health care provided to children in foster care. For example, New York City uses medical care audits to examine the quality of services provided to the 17,000 children in the city's foster care program.[57] The city reported conducting two types of medical care audits—a routine medical audit conducted every 2 years and a special medical audit for children with HIV, conducted at least annually. These reviews apply an audit tool that is based on local foster care standards for physical and mental health to assess documentation in medical records of the child's medical history, consent for treatments, comprehensive physical examinations, diagnostic screenings, immunization history and status, developmental and behavioral health screenings, and the use of psychotropic medications. Reviewers provide their results to foster care agencies, noting findings that must be addressed immediately, as well as a corrective action plan. The audit score is incorporated into a cumulative score on the agency's performance. Officials in Illinois and Utah also reported the use of medical audits to ensure the delivery of appropriate care.

ACF Offers States Health-Related Technical Assistance as Part of Its Broader Efforts to Improve Delivery of Services

Although states are ultimately responsible for meeting the health needs of children in foster care, HHS is required by law to provide technical assistance to the extent feasible to help states develop and implement plans to improve their performance. ACF officials told us that their emphasis is on providing technical assistance that will increase the capacity of state child welfare agencies over the long term to serve the needs of children in their care. ACF officials point out that they do not expect to provide expertise in the area of health care, but instead to help child welfare agencies carry out their mission within the flexibility that states have.

ACF's 25 technical assistance centers—including one center that specializes in children's mental health—offer states a range of assistance, from on-site consultation to Web-based information on promising practices. In some cases, the centers help state child welfare agencies develop strategies to obtain needed services and coordinate their efforts with others involved in health care, such as the agencies responsible for Medicaid, public health, mental health, and substance abuse treatment.[58] These and other agencies are listed among possible stakeholders in ACF's reviews of state child welfare agencies. ACF and center staff also referred to the assistance that is available from nonfederal sources, such as universities and private foundations.[59]

Technical assistance in the form of on-site consultation is provided at state request, and few states have requested on-site consultation specifically to address health care services for children. On-site consultation generally is requested from ACF regions, coordinated through the National Child Welfare Resource Center for Organizational Improvement, and tracked by ACF through a dedicated data system. The centers we contacted generally report that they have not been asked to provide consultants on site, but have provided other forms of assistance related to the health care needs of children in foster care.[60]

Table 4 provides summary information on the centers in ACF's network that either specialize in an aspect of health care or have reported providing some assistance on health care practices through 2008, including one center with funding from HHS's SAMHSA that focuses on children's mental health.[61] Examples of some of the work these centers perform in relation to health care are discussed below.

Table 4. Centers in ACF's Training and Technical Assistance Network That Have Provided Assistance Related to Foster Children's Health Care through 2008

Name of center	Web site address	ACF funds in 2008	SAMHSA funds in 2008
Center specializing in aspects of health care			
National Technical Assistance Center for Children's Mental Health	http://gucchd.georgetown.edu/	$ 350,000[a]	$3,050,000
Centers with other responsibilities that report having assisted with health care practices			
National Resource Center for Family-Centered Practice and Permanency Planning	www.nrcfcppp.org	1,270,000	None
National Child Welfare Resource Center for Organizational Improvement	www.nrcoi.org	1,750,000	None
National Child Welfare Resource Center for Youth Development	www.nrcys.ou.edu/yd	1,250,000	None
Child Welfare Information Gateway	www.childwelfare.gov	7,982,000	None

Source: GAO analysis of ACF information.

[a] $200,000 is for assistance to recipients of a discretionary grant to implement systems of care, only some of which are state agencies.

The center that specializes in aspects of children's health care is the National Technical Assistance Center for Children's Mental Health, based at Georgetown University, which helps states and other entities build systems to improve access and outcomes for all children with mental health concerns. The center's focus is on children who have or are at risk of having emotional disorders, including children in foster care. This focus has been extended to include youth facing mental health problems who have also become involved with substance abuse. The center's services range from the development and dissemination of various publications to consultation on how to increase a state's capacity to meet children's mental health needs.[62] Specifically, at state request, center staff and consultants may work for a year or more with mental health leaders in individual states, often along with child welfare directors, to help these states identify and implement strategies to improve services for children. One staff position at the center has been reserved for a consultant with child welfare expertise. According to center staff, the center provides this type of consultation to an average of 8 to10 states each year and has served 22 states through 2008.[63] To reach more agency personnel, the center holds a training institute every other year for approximately 2,000 to 2,500 attendees that in 2008 offered a series of sessions on partnerships between mental health and child welfare agencies for assessment, early intervention and treatment, support services, and care coordination, among other topics. In carrying out their work, center officials reported coordinating closely with other federally funded centers and organizations, state professional associations, private foundations, and research groups.[64] While currently focused primarily on mental health, the center is also concerned with the integration of primary care and mental health, and prior to implementation of the ACF reviews, received funds from the Maternal and Child Health Bureau of HHS's HRSA to examine promising approaches to providing the full range of health care services for children in foster care. A series of reports were published detailing these approaches that continue to be available through this and other technical centers for use by child welfare agencies in improving their service delivery.[65]

In several other centers, staff described information that they have provided on health care practices, including the following examples:

- Seven audio conferences on topics, such as the use of psychotropic medications, assessing and treating children up through age 3, and other issues concerning the mental health of children in foster care were developed by the National Resource Center for Family-Centered Practice and Permanency Planning at New York's Hunter College School of Social Work. Among many sample areas of technical assistance, the center lists health and mental health issues for children and youth in foster care, and to that end, hosts a Webpage devoted to health care with multiple links to other relevant sites.

- Sessions regarding the role of clinics dedicated to assessing and treating children in foster care and the options for financing mental health care were featured at the 2007 annual conference for child welfare agency staff arranged by the National Child Welfare Resource Center for Organizational Improvement at the University of Maine.
- The sharing of information on the steps states are taking to extend Medicaid coverage to older youth when they leave foster care is a key area of focus for the National Child Welfare Resource Center for Youth Development in Oklahoma. The center connects states that have been successful in this area with states asking for assistance and maintains a list serve for state child welfare agency officials who are responsible for helping youth prepare for independence.

ACF regional and central office staff may also share promising practices that they observe during reviews of state programs. These practices are posted to an ACF Web site and include several related to child and family wellbeing.[66] ACF's Web site notes that the Children's Bureau does not make any representations pertaining to the effectiveness of the posted approaches, and ACF officials stated they had taken no further steps to share them and that they had not evaluated specific state practices. Other practices have been shared among states at regional meetings, as in ACF Region VII, where Kansas shared information on its medical passport. Regional staff may also share information on various practices adopted by states within the regions. For example, ACF reported that regional staff members have shared strategies for meeting children's dental needs, such as using hygienists in Kansas and using a traveling dental van in Missouri. Florida officials reported that they received assistance from ACF on referrals to early intervention programs. New York and Utah officials also acknowledged the help that they received from regional ACF staff.[67]

To assist in states' efforts to implement improvement strategies, ACF newly funded five centers in fall 2008 that are expected to provide in-depth, long-term consultation and support to states to improve the quality and effectiveness of their child welfare services starting in July 2009. ACF expects the assistance to help build partnerships to deliver a broad array of integrated services that can be individually tailored to meet the diverse needs of children and families served by child welfare agencies, including their physical, mental, and developmental needs as appropriate. As with the older centers, states' identification of needs and potential strategies will determine the assistance provided. Some assistance with aspects of health care may be available from these centers if states request it, according to ACF officials.

AGENCY COMMENTS AND OUR EVALUATION

We provided a draft of this chapter to the Department of Health and Human Services for comment and received a written response, which is included in this chapter as appendix II. HHS provided some additional information on its technical assistance to state foster care agencies, particularly through collaboration between ACF and SAMHSA, to assist states in addressing mental health and substance abuse issues among foster children. The agency also provided technical comments, which we have incorporated as appropriate.

Sincerely yours,

Kay C. Brown

Kay Brown, Director
Education, Workforce
and Income Security Issues

Cynthia A Bascetta

Cynthia A. Bascetta, Director
Health Care Issues

APPENDIX I: SELECTION OF STATES AND PRACTICES FOR GAO REVIEW

Our study had four objectives. These included describing practices that selected states have adopted to address the challenges of (1) identifying health care needs, (2) ensuring delivery of appropriate health services, and (3) documenting and monitoring the health care of children in foster care. In addition, we describe technical assistance the Department of Health and Human Services' Administration for Children and Families (ACF) provides to states to help improve their performance in providing for the health care needs of these children.

To gain an initial understanding of the types of practices states have adopted, we reviewed relevant reports and interviewed various experts and researchers. We reviewed information on promising practices listed on ACF's Web site that were identified during ACF's reviews of state performance and a list of state practices that ACF provided to us. We also interviewed several prominent child welfare experts and researchers, including individuals affiliated with the American Academy of Pediatrics, the Center for Health Care Strategies, the Chapin Hall Center for Children, the Georgetown University Child Development Center, and the National Academy for State Health Policy to obtain additional information on practices to improve the delivery of health care to children in foster care.

To update information on practices described in available publications and to obtain additional examples that may not have been reported in publications, we e-mailed requests for information on current practices they believed were noteworthy efforts to address children's health care needs to representatives of child welfare agencies in 50 states and the District of Columbia. To minimize the burden on state representatives, we suggested that they could limit the number of practices they described. We sent our e-mail requests in October 2007, and representatives for 42 of the 51 child welfare agencies provided responses.

To gather more detailed examples of these practices, we selected 10 state child welfare agencies for further review—conducting visits to 3 states and telephone interviews with 7. In selecting states and their practices for further review, we considered descriptions of each state's practices obtained from the states and other research. For practical reasons, in order to collect sufficient examples from each category while limiting the number of distinct states we would contact, we also considered whether a state had more than one practice it considered noteworthy and whether it encompassed practices in at least two of our five broad categories. We also gave some weight to the level of context and information the state had provided about its practices and generally limited our consideration of practices to those that states indicated they had begun to implement. In addition, we made efforts to include states that had achieved a strong rating on the ACF reviews for children's physical and mental health indicators and to achieve some distribution in geographic location and administrative structure.

For 3 of the 10 states selected—Illinois, New York, and Utah—we conducted site visits and interviewed officials of state child welfare agencies and state Medicaid Offices, and when possible, health care providers, interest groups, and foster care parents. For seven states—California, Delaware, Florida, Massachusetts, Oklahoma, Texas, and Washington—we conducted interviews by telephone with officials of each state's child welfare agency and, in some instances, officials of state Medicaid Offices.

Key characteristics of the selected states are shown in table 5. Collectively, the states we contacted account for 53 percent of federal IV-E funds distributed in fiscal year 2007.

For our visits and telephone interviews, we developed semistructured interview guides for state and local child welfare agencies, including caseworkers, state Medicaid offices, interest groups, and foster parents. In addition, we obtained from officials of state child welfare agencies detailed information on their identified practices, including the dates of operation; numbers of children served; size of jurisdiction covered; variety of services offered; funding mechanisms used; outcomes, if any, reported; and whether any evaluative studies had been conducted or other documents prepared that discussed the effectiveness of the practice.

We conducted our work from November 2007 to January 2009 in accordance with all sections of GAO's Quality Assurance Framework that are relevant to our objectives. The framework requires that we plan and perform the engagement to obtain sufficient and appropriate evidence to meet our stated objectives and to discuss any limitations in our work. We believe that the information and data obtained, and the analysis conducted, provide a reasonable basis for any findings and conclusions.

Table 5. Characteristics of States Contacted for GAO's Review

States GAO selected	Foster care caseload Sept. 30, 2007	Federal foster care funds 2007 (IV-E)	State match required for IV E and XIX	Federal child welfare Services funds 2007 (IV-B1)	Type of child Welfare administration	Medicaid included in same State agency as child welfare	Public, maternal & child health in same agency as child welfare	Strength in physical health Per ACF review	Strength in mental health per ACF review
Sites visited									
Ill.	16,000	$199,758,813	50.00	$11,343,733	State	No	No	No	No
NY	30,548	370,648,137	50.00	14,424,182	County	No	No	Yes	No
Utah	2,600	19,232,449	29.86	3,368,524	State	No	No	Yes	Yes
Sites contacted by teleconference									
Calif.	78,282	1,302,357,112	50.00	33,565,519	County	Yes	Yes	Yes	No
Del.	970	$5,737,528	50.00	783,771	State	No	Yes	Yes	Yes
Fla.	26,124	152,407,545	41.24	15,930,592	County	No	No	No	No
Mass.	10,000	64,838,028	50.00	4,094,353	State	Yes	No	No	No
Okla.	12,200	42,892,775	31.26	1,891,061	State	No	No	No	No
Tex.	18,000	216,799,611	39.22	25,115,256	State	Yes	Yes	No	No
Wash.	11,015	84,681,985	49.88	5,313,865	State	Yes	Yes	No	No
Total		**$4,669,165,598**							

Source: GAO analysis of federal and state child welfare data.

APPENDIX II: COMMENTS FROM THE DEPARTMENT OF HEALTH AND HUMAN SERVICES

DEPARTMENT OF HEALTH & HUMAN SERVICES OFFICE OF THE SECRETARY

Legislation

Assistant Secretary for
Washington, DC 20201

JAN 1 2 2009

Kay E. Brown, Director
Education, Workforce, and
Income Security Issues
U.S. Government Accountability Office
441 G Street NW
Washington, DC 20548

Dear Ms. Brown:

Enclosed are the Department's comments on the U.S. Government Accountability Office's (GAO) draft report entitled: "Foster Care: State Practices for Assessing Health Needs, Facilitating Service Delivery, and Monitoring Children's Care (GAO-09-26).

The Department appreciates the opportunity to review and comment on this report before its publication.

Sincerely,

Jennifer R. Luong
for Craig Burton
Acting Assistant Secretary for Legislation

Attachment

DEPARTMENT OF HEALTH & HUMAN SERVICES

ADMINISTRATION FOR CHILDREN AND FAMILIES
Office of the Assistant Secretary, Suite 600
370 L'Enfant Promenade, S.W.
Washington, D.C. 20447

JAN 0 9 2009

TO: Vincent J. Ventimiglia, Jr.
Assistant Secretary for Legislation

FROM: Daniel C. Schneider
Acting Assistant Secretary
for Children and Families

SUBJECT: Government Accountability Office (GAO) Draft Report Titled, "FOSTER CARE: State Practices for Assessing Health Needs, Facilitating Service Delivery, and Monitoring Children's Care" (GAO-09-26)

Attached are comments of the Administration for Children and Families and the Substance Abuse and Mental Health Services Administration on the above-referenced report.

Should you have questions or need additional information, please contact Christine Calpin, Associate Commissioner, Children's Bureau, Administration on Children, Youth and Families, at 202-205-8618.

Attachment

COMMENTS OF THE ADMINISTRATION FOR CHILDREN AND FAMILIES AND THE SUBSTANCE ABUSE AND MENTAL HEALTH SERVICES ADMINISTRATION ON THE GOVERNMENT ACCOUNTABILITY OFFICE DRAFT REPORT TITLED, "FOSTER CARE: STATE PRACTICES FOR ASSESSING HEALTH NEEDS, FACILITATING SERVICE DELIVERY, AND MONITORING CHILDREN'S CARE" (GAO-09-26)

The Administration for Children and Families (ACF) and the Substance Abuse and Mental Health Services Administration (SAMHSA) appreciate the opportunity to comment on the Government Accountability Office (GAO) draft report.

GAO Recommendations

GAO did not make any recommendations in this report.

In describing the National Technical Assistance Center for Children's Mental Health (Georgetown), GAO did not mention that part of the funding for this center (i.e., $150,000) comes from an Interagency Agreement with ACF. The report states, "One staff position at the center has been reserved for a consultant with child welfare expertise." This is accomplished through the Interagency Agreement between SAMHSA and ACF. This should be stated.

There is no mention that the SAMHSA-funded Technical Assistance Partnership also has a staff position for a child welfare consultant that provides assistance to SAMHSA-funded system of care communities that are part of the Comprehensive Community Mental Health for Children and Their Families Program. This staff position is similarly funded through an Interagency Agreement with ACF in the amount of $200,000, which makes the total Interagency Agreement $350,000. This position and the relationship established with ACF has allowed SAMHSA to prioritize services and consultation related to child welfare issues.

As a result of the collaboration between SAMHSA and ACF, and the significant mental health needs of foster children, SAMHSA has made the child welfare population a priority in the Request for Application (RFA) used to solicit proposals for the Comprehensive Community Mental Health for Children and Their Families Program. Specifically, page 2 of the RFA states that applicants are encouraged to address children and youth involved with the child welfare system. Creating priority status for children and youth in the child welfare system has resulted in a number of grantees that specifically focus on foster children, which has helped create collaborations and partnerships between mental health and child welfare systems in States and communities across the nation. Of the 59 currently funded system of care grantees, 7 have a primary focus on foster children.

While SAMHSA manages this Center, ACF is a significant fund provider of the Center's activities. Similar to the other technical assistance centers funded by ACF, NCSACW does not provide direct medical services, but provides assistance to agencies supporting positive child welfare outcomes.

NCSACW completed a review of the Round 1 Child and Family Services Reviews (CFSRs) and Program Improvement Plans, managed by ACF, and found that 13 of the States specifically mentioned that services were inadequate to meet the substance abuse treatment needs of adolescents in their caseloads. Although not specifically mentioned in reports from other States, this is likely to be a much more widely experienced problem.

Related GAO Products

Medicare Physician Payment: Care Coordination Programs Used in Demonstration Show Progress, but Wider Use of Payment Approach May Be Limited. GAO-08-65. Washington, D.C.: February 15, 2008.

Department of Health and Human Services, Centers for Medicare and Medicaid Services: Medicaid Program; Elimination of Reimbursement Under Medicaid for School Administration Expenditures and Costs Related to Transportation of School-Age Children Between Home and School. GAO-08-394R. Washington, D.C.: January 11, 2008.

Child Welfare: Additional Federal Action Could Help States Address Challenges in Providing Services to Children and Families. GAO-07-850T. Washington, D.C.: May 15, 2007.

Medicaid: Concerns Remain about Sufficiency of Data for Oversight of Children's Dental Services. GAO-07-826T. Washington, D.C.: May 2, 2007.

Pediatric Drug Research: Studies Conducted Under Best Pharmaceuticals for Children Act. GAO-07-557. Washington, D.C.: March 22, 2007.

Children's Health Insurance: States' SCHIP Enrollment and Spending and Considerations for Reauthorization. GAO-07-558T. Washington, D.C.: March 1, 2007.

Child Welfare: Improving Social Service Program, Training, and Technical Assistance Information Would Help Address Long-standing Service-Level and Workforce Challenges. GAO-07-75. Washington, D.C.: October 6, 2006.

Foster Care and Adoption Assistance: Federal Oversight Needed to Safeguard Funds and Ensure Consistent Support for States' Administrative Costs. GAO-06-649. Washington, D.C.: June 15, 2006.

Administrative Expenditures and Federal Matching Rates of Selected Support Programs. GAO-05-839R. Washington, D.C.: June 30, 2005.

Medicaid Financing: States' Use of Contingency-Fee Consultants to Maximize Federal Reimbursements Highlights Need for Improved Federal Oversight. GAO-05-748. Washington, D.C.: June 28, 2005.

Medicaid: States' Efforts to Maximize Federal Reimbursements Highlight Need for Improved Federal Oversight. GAO-05-836T. Washington, D.C.: June 28, 2005.

Child And Family Services Reviews: States and HHS Face Challenges in Assessing and Improving State Performance. GAO-04-781T. Washington, D.C.: May 13, 2004.

Child And Family Services Reviews: Better Use of Data and Improved Guidance Could Enhance HHS's Oversight of State Performance. GAO-04-333. Washington, D.C.: April 20, 2004.

Medicaid and SCHIP: States' Premium and Cost Sharing Requirements for Beneficiaries. GAO-04-491. Washington, D.C.: March 30, 2004.

SCHIP: HHS Continues to Approve Waivers That Are Inconsistent with Program Goals. GAO-04-166R. Washington, D.C.: January 5, 2004.

Child Welfare: States Face Challenges in Developing Information Systems and Reporting Reliable Child Welfare Data. GAO-04-267T. Washington, D.C.: November 19, 2003.

Child Welfare: Most States Are Developing Statewide Information Systems, but the Reliability of Child Welfare Data Could Be Improved. GAO-03-809. Washington, D.C.: July 31, 2003.

Child Welfare and Juvenile Justice: Federal Agencies Could Play a Stronger Role in Helping States Reduce the Number of Children Placed Solely to Obtain Mental Health Services. GAO-03-397. Washington, D.C.: April 21, 2003.

Medicaid and SCHIP: States Use Varying Approaches to Monitor Children's Access to Care. GAO-03-222. Washington, D.C.: January 14, 2003.

Mental Health Services: Effectiveness of Insurance Coverage and Federal Programs for Children Who Have Experienced Trauma Largely Unknown. GAO-02-813. Washington, D.C.: August 22, 2002.

Medicaid and SCHIP: States' Enrollment and Payment Policies Can Affect Children's Access to Care. GAO-01-883. Washington, D.C.: September 10, 2001.

Medicaid: Stronger Efforts Needed to Ensure Children's Access to Health Screening Services. GAO-01-749. Washington, D.C.: July 13, 2001.

Foster Care: Health Needs of Many Young Children Are Unknown And Unmet. GAO/HEHS-95-114. Washington, D.C.: May 26, 1995.

End Notes

[1] Medicaid is a federal-state health financing program established in 1965 to provide health care coverage to certain categories of low-income adults and children.

[2] For example, federal law requires that states have standards to ensure children in foster care are provided quality services to protect their safety and health. In addition, states must maintain case plans for children that include health records, including the most recent information available regarding their immunizations, known medical problems, medications, and their health providers' names and addresses.

[3] Pub. L. No. 110-351 (2008).

[4] Throughout the report, we use the term "health" to refer to both physical and mental health. Physical health includes dental health. Other health areas included are those dealing with children's development and with substance abuse.

[5] As part of our process to select states, we asked all state child welfare agencies to identify some practices that they had adopted and considered noteworthy to screen and assess needs, facilitate and coordinate access to care, or manage data and information. We received 42 responses. While most of the 10 states reported having multiple practices, we did not cover all of these practices adopted by each state.

[6] While states have primary responsibility for the welfare of children in their care, this responsibility has been delegated to county agencies in about one-fifth of the states, including many of the nation's most populous states such as California, Florida, and New York.

[7] Data for federal fiscal year 2006 were the most recent available. The proportion of children who meet federal eligibility criteria has decreased over the past decade since the income criteria are set at the 1996 income levels under the former Aid to Families with Dependent Children program. See GAO, *Foster Care and Adoption Assistance: Federal Oversight Needed to Safeguard Funds and Ensure Consistent Support for States' Administrative Costs,* GAO-06-649 (Washington, D.C.: June 15, 2006).

[8] Included are IV-E funds available to states to reimburse up to 50 percent of their IV-E administrative costs for child placement, information systems, and other purposes and up to 75 percent of their IV-E training costs. (45 C.F.R. § 1356.60(b) and (c))

[9] States may also use other federal funds, such as the title XX Social Services Block Grant or Temporary Assistance to Needy Families, to provide some child welfare services.

[10] Title IV-B includes two different programs: subpart 1 for general child welfare services and subpart 2 for family preservation, family support, time-limited family reunification, and adoption promotion and support services. Some of the funds available under subpart 2 may be used for health care services, such as counseling, mental health, and substance abuse treatment for foster children or their families, during the 15 months following the children's entry into foster care in order to facilitate the timely, safe reunification of these foster children with their families.

[11] Child and Family Services Improvement Act of 2006, Pub. L. No. 109-288 (2006).

[12] Fostering Connections to Success and Increasing Adoptions Act of 2008, Pub. L. No. 110-351 (2008). ACF alerted states to this new requirement but did not issue further instructions in 2008.

[13] ACF's reviews examined a sample of the case records of children served by state agencies; children in foster care, the focus of GAO's work, were a subset of this sample.

[14] In the initial round of CFSRs, ACF designated a state as showing strength when 85 percent of the up to 65 case records examined in that state indicated that the state had assessed needs and provided treatment as appropriate. Depending on the state, the results varied widely, with the percentage of sampled children who were not assessed or treated ranging from 8 percent to 49 percent. In the next round of reviews, occurring from 2007 through 2010, states will have to assess and treat 90 percent of cases examined in order to show strengths and 95 percent of cases in order to be deemed in substantial conformity.

[15] In November 2008, ACF reported that 39 states had achieved their planned goals and action steps, including those for children's health; that 7 states had missed their planned goals and action steps and were subject to withholding of federal grant funds; and that the actions of 6 states were still being evaluated. ACF withheld grant funds from one state that did not complete the action steps for improving children's health. See 45 C.F.R. § 1355.36 for regulations governing the withholding of grant funds.

[16] In addition to Medicaid, federal funds are available to states for health-related services for a population that may include children in foster care under title V of the Social Security Act for maternal and child health, under title XIX of the Public Health Service Act for community mental health centers, and under the Individuals with Disabilities Education Act.

[17] *See* 42 U.S.C. § 1396a(a)(10)(A)(i)(I).

[18] The Urban Institute reports that all states have extended Medicaid coverage to children in foster care. See Rob Geen, Anna Sommers, and Mindy Cohen, The Urban Institute, *Medicaid Spending on Foster Children* (Washington, D.C., 2005). However, some children are excluded, such as noncitizens, those with private health insurance, and children who leave foster care while they are on trial visits to their homes.

[19] This represents federal and state dollars combined for the most recent year available. Expenditures for children in foster care are likely to be underestimated and may exclude expenditures for some children participating in foster care.

[20] Fee-for-service arrangements may also include primary care case management, where primary care providers are paid a monthly, per capita case management fee, usually around $3, to coordinate care for beneficiaries, in addition to fee-for-service reimbursement for any health care services they provide. Coordination may involve referrals to specialists and other providers.

[21] *See* 42 U.S.C. §§ 1396a(a)(43), 1396d(a)(4)(B).

[22] *See* 42 C.F.R. § 441.50 et seq.

[23] For example, The Urban Institute reported that 38 states funded targeted case management under Medicaid for children in foster care. See Rob Geen, Anna Sommers, and Mindy Cohen, The Urban Institute, *Medicaid Spending on Foster Children,* (Washington, D.C., 2005*).*

[24] *See* 42 U.S.C. §§ 1396(a)(25), 1396n(g)(4).

[25] We reported that most states have used contingency-fee consultants to help implement a wide range of projects, including rehabilitative and targeted case management services, to maximize federal Medicaid reimbursements. In particular, we found that during fiscal years 1999 through 2003, combined state and federal spending for one category of Medicaid services—targeted case management—increased by 76 percent, from $1.7 billion to $3 billion, across all states. See GAO, *Medicaid Financing: States' Use of Contingency-Fee Consultants to Maximize Federal Reimbursements Highlight Need for Improved Federal Oversight,* GAO-05-748 (Washington, D.C.: June 28, 2005).

[26] The Deficit Reduction Act of 2005 amended the Social Security Act provisions concerning Medicaid coverage for case management and targeted case management services effective January 1, 2006. *See* Pub. L. No. 109-171, §6052, 120 Stat. 4, 93-95.

[27] See *Medicaid Program; Optional State Plan Case Managed Services* (72 Fed. Reg. 68077, December 4, 2007); and *Medicaid Program; Coverage for Rehabilitative Services* (72 Fed. Reg. 45201, August 13, 2007).

[28] Supplemental Appropriations Act, 2008, Pub. L. No. 110-252, §7001(a), 122 Stat. 2323, 2387-88.

[29] Organizations such as the American Academy of Pediatrics, the American Academy of Child and Adolescent Psychiatry, and the Child Welfare League of America recommend assessments for children shortly after children enter foster care. However, to avoid undue burden on children and providers, both Delaware and New York consider that assessments made prior to entry into foster care may suffice.

[30] Laurel K. Leslie, Michael S. Hurlburt, John Landsverk et al., "Comprehensive Assessments for Children Entering Foster Care: A National Perspective," *Pediatrics, 112* (1) (2003), pp. 134-142. (Accessible via http://www.pediatrics.org/cgi/content/full/112/1/134.). Also see N. Halfon, A. Zepeda, and M. Inkelas (2002), *Mental Health Services for Children in Foster Care* (Policy Brief Number 4). Los Angeles: UCLA Center for Healthier Children, Families and Communities.

[31] A.C. Stahmer, L.K. Leslie, J. A. Landsverk et al., "Developmental Services for Young Children in Foster Care: Assessment and Service Delivery," *Journal of Social Service Research,* 33 (2) (2006), pp. 27-38.

[32] Florida requires the initial screening within 72 hours; New York recommends but does not require that its counties and agencies provide an initial screening.

[33] California has no policy on initial screenings, but some of its counties conduct examinations that are similar. Texas's contract with its health providers requires that children newborn to age 3 receive an exam within 14 days of enrollment in the health plan and that older children receive an exam within 21 days. A dental exam must be provided within 60 days for children age 1 or

older. Providers may be penalized financially if they do not meet these timelines for certain percentages of children. Washington's assessment process must be completed within 30 days of entry into foster care for children who are expected to remain in out-of-home placement longer than 30 days.

[34] Such a policy may involve separate child welfare and Medicaid requirements. For example, Massachusetts officials indicated that the state child welfare agency has a policy specifying that foster parents schedule and support subsequent health care screenings of the foster children in their care. The Massachusetts Medicaid agency requires that Medicaid providers perform ongoing screenings which follow the standards set by the state Medicaid agency for EPSDT screens.

[35] See Administration for Children and Families, Office of Planning, Research, and Evaluation, *National Survey of Child and Adolescent Well-Being Research Brief No. 7: Special Health Care Needs among Children in Child Welfare, Research Brief, Findings from the NSCAW Study* (2008).

[36] See Jan McCarthy and others, National Technical Assistance Center for Children's Mental Health and Technical Assistance Partnership for Child, and Family Mental Health, *Child and Family Services Reviews 2001-2004—A Mental Health Analysis* (Washington, D.C., August 2007), p. 14.

[37] See P. K. Jaudes, L. A. Bilaver, R. M. George and others, "Improving Access to Health Care for Foster Children: The Illinois Model," *Child Welfare*, 83 (3) (2004), 215-238; and S. M. Horowitz, P. Owens, and M. D. Simms, "Specialized Assessments for Children in Foster Care," *Pediatrics,* 106 (2000), 59-66 (available at http://www.pediatrics.org/cgi/content/full/106/1/59, accessed on November 18, 2008).

[38] P. K. Jaudes and others "Improving Access to Health Care for Foster Children: The Illinois Model," *Child Welfare*, 83 (3) (2004), 215-238.

[39] See L. K. Leslie and others "Comprehensive Assessments for Children Entering Foster Care: A National Perspective", *Pediatrics*, 112 (1)(2003), pp. 134-142. (Accessible via http://www.pediatrics.org/cgi/content/full/112/1/134.), or S. M. Horowitz, P. Owens, and M.D. Simms, "Specialized Assessments for Children in Foster Care," *Pediatrics,* 106 (2000), 59-66 (available at http://www.pediatrics.org/cgi/content/full/106/1/59, accessed on November 18, 2008).

[40] State officials reported that in 2008, the agency funded 45 full-time equivalent social worker positions to assess children, with at least one social worker in each of the state's 44 child welfare offices. Each social worker was responsible for assessing approximately 12 to 14 children each month and entering the results into the state's child welfare case management system.

[41] For all children covered by Medicaid, not just those in foster care, state officials told us that Illinois also has a performance payment of $30 per child per year if a required number of visits is met, as well as an expedited payment process that returns payment within 30 days. Additionally, the state was implementing a pay-for-performance bonus for serving a certain number of children.

[42] Telepsychiatry is a form of video conferencing that can facilitate provision of psychiatric services to patients living in remote locations or otherwise underserved areas.

[43] Rebecca Colman and others, *The New York State Care Coordination Pilot Project: Process and Impact Evaluation Study Findings*, a report for the New York State Office of Children and Family Services, March 2007.

[44] State officials told us the 2008 budget for the nursing program is approximately $3.1 million. The majority of costs are personnel costs, with about 46 percent paid for by federal Medicaid funds, 18 percent by state health department funds, and 36 percent by state child welfare department funds. These funds are used to provide services for up to 2,600 children enrolled in foster care on any given day.

[45] The two medical care management agencies in Cook County that do not use the reminder-recall system are local health departments.

[46] Colman et. al., *The New York State Care Coordination Pilot Project: Process and Impact Evaluation Study Findings*, a report for the New York State Office of Children and Family Services, March 2007.

[47] Psychotropic medications may have more than one purpose and may be used to treat other medical conditions. For example, the same drug may be used to control seizures for someone with epilepsy and to reduce mood swings in someone with bipolar disorder.

[48] Diane L. Green, Wesley Hawkins, and Michelle Hawkins, "Medication of Children and Youth in Foster Care," *Disability Issues for Social Workers and Human Services Professionals in the Twenty-First Century*, (New York: Haworth Press, 2005). Also see GAO, *Pediatric Drug Research: Studies Conducted under Best Pharmaceuticals for Children Act*, GAO-07-557 (Washington, D.C.: Mar. 22, 2007).

[49] Julie M. Zito and others, "Psychotropic Medication Patterns Among Youth in Foster Care," *Pediatrics*, vol. 121, no. 1 (2008): e157-e163.

[50] The types of circumstances cited include the absence of a clinical diagnosis, the concurrent use of five or more psychotropic medications, multiple medications being used before trying just one, exceeding the usually recommended dose, and prescribing psychotropic medications for children less than 4 years of age.

[51] See http://www.hhsc.state.tx.us/medicaid/occ/Psychoactive_Medications.html (accessed on Sept. 2, 2008).

[52] The passport covers children in foster care placements, children placed with relatives by the state, children formerly in the foster care program who have returned home but remain in the state's custody, and children who voluntarily entered into the state's care.

[53] See the following Web site for further information: https://www.fostercaretx. com/ portal/public/fc/fostercare/health.

[54] The Congressional Budget Office recently noted that electronic health records in general might help with the sharing of health information, which in turn might improve the quality of care. See Congressional Budget Office, *Evidence on the Costs and Benefits of Health Information Technology* (May 2008).

[55] Department of Health and Human Services, Office of Inspector General, *State Medicaid Agencies' Initiatives on Health Information Technology and Health Information Exchange,* OEI-02-06-00270 (Washington, D.C., August 2007).

[56] See the Department of Health and Human Services, Administration for Children and Families Web site, Summary of the Results of the 2001-2004 Child and Family Services Reviews, *General Findings from The Federal Child and Family Services Review*, p. 17 of 39. This is available at http://www.acf.hhs.gov/programs/cb/cwmonitoring/results/index.htm (accessed on Aug. 28, 2008).

[57] According to New York officials, as of February 2008, New York City's foster care population represented more than 80 percent of all children in the foster care system in the state.

[58] In commenting on a draft of this chapter, HHS officials noted that ACF uses an interagency agreement with the Substance Abuse and Mental Health Services Administration to contribute to an additional technical assistance center called the "*National Center on Substance Abuse and Child Welfare*." While GAO's research identified this additional center, the mission of the center focused on substance use in intact families and did not specifically address foster children; therefore, this center was not included in the scope of the GAO study.

[59] Several of the centers include links to the websites of these other organizations. For example, the National Resource Center for Family-Centered Practice and Permanency Planning Center provides a link to The Commonwealth Fund for information on developmental screening.

[60] The centers submit regular reports to ACF on their activities, but they do not have to identify the particular assistance provided individual states. On-site consultation to individual states, however, must be reported by eight centers through the Technical Assistance Tracking Internet System. As GAO has previously reported, ACF has not independently evaluated the centers' effectiveness.

[61] The National Center on Substance Abuse and Child Welfare, operated by the Center for Children and Family Futures, is charged with assisting states and others to improve outcomes for families with substance use disorders who are involved in the child welfare and family court systems.

[62] An example of the center's recent publications is: *Child and Family Services Reviews 2001-2004 - A Mental Health Analysis, 2007,* which reports on mental health service delivery challenges and management trends noted in ACF reviews and state improvement plans.

[63] The 22 states are Alaska, Arizona, Arkansas, Florida, Georgia, Illinois, Indiana, Kentucky, Maryland, Minnesota, Mississippi, Missouri, Nebraska, Nevada, New Hampshire, New Mexico, Oklahoma, Pennsylvania, South Carolina, Tennessee, Utah, and Vermont.

[64] The center has worked closely with the Technical Assistance Partnership for Child and Family Mental Health operated by the American Institutes for Research with SAMHSA funding, the National Association of State Mental Health Program Directors, The Annie E. Casey Foundation, and the University of South Florida.

[65] See *Meeting the Health Care Needs of Children in the Foster Care System*, 2002, an HRSA-sponsored publication that reported on a 3-year study of promising approaches to meeting the physical, mental, emotional, developmental, and dental health needs of foster children.

[66] See http://www.acf.hhs.gov/programs/cb/cwmonitoring/promise/index.htm (accessed on Nov. 21, 2008).

[67] For more information on ACF's technical assistance and states' reactions, see GAO, *Child and Family Services Reviews: Better Use of Data Could Enhance HHS's Oversight of State Performance,* GAO-04-333 (Washington, D.C.: Apr. 20, 2004).

In: Foster Care and African-American Youth
Editor: Joanna Kaczmarek
ISBN: 978-1-60741-541-1

Chapter 3

CHILD WELFARE: HHS ACTIONS WOULD HELP STATES PREPARE YOUTH IN THE FOSTER CARE SYSTEM FOR INDEPENDENT LIVING*

United States Government Accountability Office

WHAT GAO DID THIS STUDY

Congress passed the Foster Care Independence Act of 1999 (FCIA), which doubled annual federal funds for independent living programs to $140 million. This testimony discusses (1) states' FCIA funding allocations, (2) services provided and remaining challenges, (3) state coordination of programs to deliver services, and (4) the states and the Department of Health and Human Services' (HHS) Administration for Children and Families' (ACF) progress toward meeting program accountability requirements. This testimony is primarily based on our 2004 report on FCIA (05-25), with updated information from our 2007 testimony on state child welfare challenges (07-850T). To conduct the 2004 work, we surveyed state independent living coordinators, conducted 4 state site visits, and reviewed states' plans and annual reports. Updated information from our 2007 testimony was taken primarily from a 2006 survey of state child welfare directors.

* This is an edited, reformatted and augmented version of a U. S. Government Accountability Office publication dated July 2007.

What GAO Recommends

We recommended that HHS improve access to federal program information. HHS did not comment on this recommendation in 2004, but disagreed with a similar recommendation in our 2007 testimony. We also recommended that HHS improve its state monitoring processes. HHS agreed to develop uniform monitoring tools, but disagrees that standard state reports are necessary.

What GAO Found

States' funding allocations for independent living programs effectively ranged from a maximum of approximately $500 to $2,300 for each foster care youth who was eligible for independent living services, according to data available at the time of our 2004 report. Funding varied because of differences in states' eligibility requirements and the funding formula used to allocate funds.

Although our 2004 survey of state independent living coordinators showed that 40 states reported expanding existing independent living services to younger youth and 36 states reported serving youth older than they had previously served, states varied in their ability to engage youth and to provide key services. About one-third of reporting states were serving less than half of their eligible foster care youth population, while an equal percentage of states were serving three-fourths or more. Our 2006 survey of state child welfare directors showed that critical gaps remain in providing services such as mental health and housing for youth transitioning to independence. Mental health barriers included differences in eligibility requirements and level of services between the youth and adult systems, and long waiting lists. Housing barriers included limited affordable housing in costly urban areas, scarce rental housing in rural areas, and problems obtaining a rental lease due to the lack of youth employment and credit history or a co-signer to guarantee payment.

Almost all states that we surveyed in 2004 reported an increase in coordination with some federal, state, and local programs, but linkages with other federal and state youth-serving programs were not always in place to increase services available across local areas. Many programs exist at the federal, state, or local level that can be used to provide or supplement independent living services, and each state reported in our survey using some of these programs to provide services. Despite these coordination efforts, some states may not make full use of the available resources. Inconsistent availability of information on the array of programs that were operating in each state and local area was cited as a challenge in promoting coordination in both our prior and more current work.

States and HHS have taken action to fulfill the accountability provisions of FCIA, but 8 years later, little information is available to assess program outcomes. All states developed multiyear plans for their programs and submitted annual reports, but using these documents to assess state performance was hindered by inconsistencies between the plans and reports, an absence of goals and baseline information to measure progress, and incomplete information on outcomes for the youth serviced. ACF started developing an information system in 2000 to monitor state performance, but final regulations directing states to begin collecting data and tracking outcomes are still pending. ACF is also conducting evaluations of selected independent living programs, but results are not yet available.

Mr. Chairman and Members of the Subcommittee:

Thank you for inviting me here today to discuss the needs of youth who leave the foster care system each year without the support of an adoptive or other permanent home. As you are aware, almost 40 percent of the estimated 513,000 children in foster care are age 13 or older, and over 24,000 youth left the foster care system in 2005 as emancipated youth without a permanent living arrangement. Research studies have shown that many of these young people face serious problems once on their own, including homelessness, a lack of education and stable employment, and difficulties obtaining medical and mental health services. In response to concerns that youth leave foster care poorly prepared to live self-sufficiently, in 1986 Congress created the Independent Living Program, which was further strengthened with the passage of the Foster Care Independence Act of 1999 (FCIA) and creation of the John H. Chafee Foster Care Independence Program (Chafee Program). Under the new program, overall federal funding doubled for independent living programs from $70 million to $140 million.[1] In addition to providing increased funding, FCIA resulted in other significant changes for the independent living program.

My testimony today will focus on four key issues as they relate to the implementation of the Chafee Program:

1. how states' funding allocations for independent living programs compare when considering the number of youth eligible for services,
2. the extent to which states have expanded independent living services and age groups for youth in foster care after the passage of FCIA and what challenges remain,

3. the extent to which states have used other federal and state programs to coordinate the delivery of independent living services to foster care youth, and
4. how the states and the Department of Health and Human Services (HHS) have fulfilled the program accountability provisions of the law and assessed the effectiveness of independent living services.

My comments are based on the findings of a report GAO issued in 2004,[2] with updated information from a May 2007 testimony on challenges facing state child welfare systems.[3] The information reported in the 2004 report was based on survey responses from independent living coordinators in all 50 states and the District of Columbia regarding their experiences in developing and implementing their Chafee Programs in federal fiscal year 2003. Where appropriate, we compared those responses to information we gathered on state independent living programs operating in federal fiscal year 1998. We analyzed federal financial and foster care data. We also analyzed Chafee Program plans from 49 states, the District of Columbia, and Puerto Rico for 2001-2004, and 90 annual progress and services reports for 2001 and 2002. We visited 4 states—Connecticut, Florida, Texas, and Washington—and two local areas within each state, where we spoke with state and local officials, caseworkers, youth, foster parents, and contract providers. Finally, we interviewed HHS officials, federal contractors, and child welfare experts, and reviewed relevant documents and literature. We included updated information—taken primarily from our 2006 survey of state child welfare directors—from our 2007 testimony on challenges states face in improving outcomes for children. In addition, we included additional information from reports issued by the American Public Human Services Association, the Congressional Research Service, and the National Resource Center for Youth Services. We conducted our work in accordance with generally accepted government auditing standards.

In summary,

- States' funding allocations for independent living programs effectively ranged from a maximum of approximately $500 to $2,300 for each foster care youth who was eligible for independent living services, according to data available at the time of our 2004 report. Funding varied because of differences in states' eligibility requirements and the funding formula used to allocate funds.
- Although our 2004 survey of state independent living coordinators showed that 40 states reported expanding existing independent living

services to younger youth and 36 states reported serving youth older than they had previously served, states varied in their ability to engage youth and to provide key services. About one-third of reporting states were serving less than half of their eligible foster care youth population, while an equal percentage of states were serving three-fourths or more, and states we visited reported that gaps in the availability of critical services contributed to the differences in proportion of youth served. For example, securing safe and secure housing was identified as a challenge by youth and program officials in the 4 states we visited, including limited affordable housing in costly urban areas and scarce rental housing in rural areas. In addition, our more recent survey of state child welfare directors in 2006 showed that 31 states remained dissatisfied with housing for youth transitioning to independence, and similar numbers of states were dissatisfied with the availability of mental health, substance abuse, and dental health services.

- Almost all states that we surveyed in 2004 reported an increase in coordination with some federal, state, and local programs, but linkages with other federal and state youth-serving programs were not always in place to increase services available across local areas. Many programs exist at the federal, state, or local level that can be used to provide or supplement independent living services, and each state reported in our survey using some of these programs to provide services. Despite these coordination efforts, some states may not make full use of the available resources. Inconsistent availability of information on the array of programs that were operating in each state and local area was cited as a challenge in promoting coordination in both our prior and more current work.
- States and HHS have taken action to fulfill the accountability provisions of FCIA, but little information is available to assess the effectiveness of independent living services. At the time of our review in 2004, all states had developed their initial multiyear plans for their programs and submitted annual reports to the Administration for Children and Families (ACF), but using these plans and the reports to assess state performance was hindered by inconsistencies between the plans and reports, an absence of goals and baseline information to use in measuring progress, and incomplete information on outcomes for all youth who received services. Although in 2000 ACF began taking steps to develop an information system that will allow it to capture data on the characteristics, services, and outcomes of youth in independent living

programs, it has not yet implemented the final regulations directing states to begin collecting data and tracking outcomes. ACF is also conducting an evaluation of selected independent living programs.

In our 2004 report, we recommended that the Secretary of HHS improve the availability of information on the array of federal programs that could be used to assist youth transitioning out of foster care. HHS did not comment on this recommendation. Our 2007 testimony cites a similar recommendation that HHS take action to improve awareness of and access to federal social services by such means as modifying the Catalog of Federal Domestic Assistance. HHS disagreed with this recommendation, stating that it was insufficient to address the problem and incorrectly implied that caseworkers were not already aware of existing resources. We continue to support the recommendation based on the results of our work.

Our 2004 report also recommended that HHS improve existing processes for monitoring states' progress in meeting the needs of current and former foster care youth by developing a standard reporting format for state plans and progress reports, and implementing a uniform process regional offices can use to assess states' progress in meeting the needs of youth in foster care and those recently emancipated from care. HHS continues to disagree with our recommendation to provide a standard reporting format in that it would be overly prescriptive and impose an unnecessary burden on states. In addition, HHS reported that when standard data are available through the National Youth in Transition Database, the agency would be better positioned to determine how best to assess state performance. In the continued absence of implementation of such a database, we continue to support our recommendation to monitor state performance through modification of existing state reporting requirements. HHS agreed with our recommendation to implement a uniform process that regional offices can use to assess states' progress, but has not yet done so.

BACKGROUND

In 1986, Congress amended Title IV-E of the Social Security Act to authorize federal funds targeted to assist youth aged 16 and over in making the transition from foster care to living independent of the child welfare system and created the Independent Living Program. This program was designed to prepare adolescents in foster care to live self-sufficiently once they exited the child welfare system. Several amendments were made to the Independent Living Program over the years, but the passage of FCIA and the creation of the Chafee Program represented the most significant changes in the federal Independent Living Program since its creation. FCIA doubled the federal funds available for independent living programs to $140 million each year.[4] These funds are allocated to states based on their share of the nation's foster care population.[5]

In addition to providing increased funding, FCIA eliminated the minimum age limit of 16 years and provided states with the flexibility to define the age at which children in foster care are eligible for services to help them prepare for independent living, as long as services are provided to youth who are likely to remain in foster care until 18 years of age.

The law also provided several new services to help youth make the transition to adulthood.

- It allowed states to use up to 30 percent of their state allotment for room and board for former foster care youth up to age 21.
- It allowed states the option to expand Medicaid coverage to former foster care adolescents between 18 and 21.
- Title IV-E was amended again in 2002 to provide foster care youth vouchers for postsecondary education and training under the Education and Training Vouchers (ETV) program and authorized an additional $60 million for states to provide postsecondary education and training vouchers up to $5,000 per year per youth. Eligible participants include youth otherwise eligible for services under the states' Chafee Programs, youth adopted from foster care after attaining the age of 16, and youth participating in the voucher program on their 21st birthday (until they turn 23 years old) as long as they are enrolled in a postsecondary education or training program and are making satisfactory progress toward completion of that program.

In addition, the law required that states make every effort to coordinate their Chafee Programs with other federal and state programs for youth, such as the Runaway and Homeless Youth Program, abstinence education programs, local housing programs, programs for disabled youth, and school-to-work programs offered by high schools or local workforce agencies. Further, states were required to coordinate their programs with each Indian tribe in the state and offer the state's independent living services to Indian children.

To receive funds under the Chafee Program, states were required to develop multiyear plans describing how they would design and deliver programs and to submit program certifications. The multiyear Chafee plans must include a description of the state's program design, including its goals, strategies, and its implementation plan for achieving the purposes of the law. States were also required to certify that they would operate a statewide independent living program that complied with the specific aspects of the law, such as providing training to foster parents, adoptive parents, workers in group homes, and case managers on issues confronting adolescents preparing for independent living. Further, to receive annual funds, ACF required states to submit annual reports that described the services provided and activities conducted under their Chafee Programs, including information on any program modifications and their current status of implementation; provide a record of how funds were expended; and include a description of the extent to which the funds assisted youth age 18 to 21 in making the transition to self-sufficiency.

FCIA also required that HHS develop and implement a plan to collect information needed to effectively monitor and measure a state's performance, including the characteristics of youth served by independent living programs, the services delivered, and the outcomes achieved. Further, FCIA required HHS to conduct evaluations of independent living programs deemed to be innovative or of potential national significance using rigorous scientific standards to the maximum extent practicable, such as random assignment to treatment and control groups.

FCIA Increased Independent Living Allocations for Most States and Allocations per Youth Vary by State

While overall federal funding for state independent living programs doubled with the passage of FCIA, there were significant variations in the changes to state allocations, and the maximum amount of funds available at the time of our 2004 report for each eligible foster care youth ranged between $476 and $2,300. Under the previous independent living program, states received funds ranging from $13,000 in Alaska to more than $12 million in California. In the first year of funding under FCIA, Alaska and 8 other states received the guaranteed minimum of $500,000, while California received more than $27 million (see table 1). Some states were unable to spend all of their federal allocations in the first 2 years of increased funding under the program. For example, in 2001, 20 states returned nearly $10 million in federal funding to HHS, and in 2002, 13 states returned more than $4 million. ACF regional officials reported that one reason for these unspent funds was that some states did not initially have the infrastructure in place to quickly absorb the influx of funds. Data provided in a July 2007 Congressional

Research Service memo to Congress showed that 9 states returned less than 1 percent of total Chafee funding in 2004 (see app. I).

Table 1. Changes in Funding Allocations across States since the Passage of FCIA

State	1998 allocation	2001 allocation	Percentage change over 1998 allocation
District of Columbia	$1,091,992	$1,091,992	0
Louisiana	1,358,131	1,358,131	0
New Jersey	2,297,848	2,297,848	0
New York	11,585,958	12,313,109	6
Pennsylvania	4,638,225	5,304,231	14
Alabama	1,038,490	1,288,304	24
Virginia	1,361,561	1,698,102	25
Maine	565,888	737,309	30
West Virginia	521,302	740,816	42
Mississippi	514,444	747,127	45
Wisconsin	1,554,305	2,252,837	45
Michigan	4,171,796	6,109,567	46
New Hampshire	320,326	500,000	56
Ohio	2,860,992	4,693,625	64
Kentucky	791,557	1,332,019	68
Vermont	295,633	500,000	69
Minnesota	1,142,066	2,102,991	84
Oregon	930,799	1,723,115	85
South Carolina	579,606	1,085,860	87
Rhode Island	314,840	612,710	95
Indiana	1,019,970	2,088,263	105
Montana	244,190	504,007	106
Connecticut	754,518	1,567,892	108
Colorado	825,854	1,785,766	116
California	12,481,777	27,570,079	121
Kansas	717,477	1,583,555	121
Missouri	1,295,026	2,940,120	127
New Mexico	207,149	500,000	141
Delaware	203,034	500,000	146
Washington	825,168	2,030,990	146
Texas	1,841,708	4,600,585	150
Arkansas	270,940	682,373	152
Iowa	449,966	1,134,717	152

Table 1. (Continued)

State	1998 allocation	2001 allocation	Percentage change over 1998 allocation
Maryland	1,238,095	3,143,032	154
North Carolina	1,045,349	2,650,713	154
Georgia	1,098,852	2,803,131	155
South Dakota	193,430	500,000	158
North Dakota	192,058	500,000	160
Utah	202,348	531,358	163
Nebraska	435,562	1,293,213	197
Oklahoma	620,076	1,910,598	208
Tennessee	777,838	2,523,776	224
Illinois	2,817,094	9,413,899	234
Nevada	153,647	517,800	237
Massachusetts	635,852	2,610,972	311
Idaho	107,004	500,000	367
Arizona	347,763	1,677,998	383
Florida	987,045	8,016,425	712
Wyoming	44,585	500,000	1,021
Hawaii	17,834	514,994	2,788
Alaska	13,032	500,000	3,737

Source: GAO analysis of HHS data.

Notes: As required by FCIA, no state received less than its federal fiscal year 1998 allotment under the Title IV-E Independent Living Program. Federal fiscal year 2001 was the first year states received full funding under FCIA.

Allocations do not account for unobligated or unliquidated funds.

Puerto Rico is not included in this analysis because the territory did not receive independent living funds in 1998. The 2001 allocation to Puerto Rico totaled $1,814,052.

At the time of our 2004 report, we could not determine the exact amount of funding states had available to spend on each youth eligible for independent living services because of the lack of data on eligible youth emancipated from foster care. However, available data at that time on youth in foster care suggest that states may have different amounts of funds available for services to youth in foster care. We compared each state's 2004 FCIA allocation with its 2002 population of eligible youth in foster care.[6] This comparison showed that maximum funding for independent living services ranged from $476 per foster care youth in West Virginia to almost $2,300 per foster care youth in Montana.[7] These differences were due in part to the new provision that allowed states to define the age ranges within which youth were eligible for independent living services. For example, 4 states reported in our survey offering independent living services to youth at age 12, while 27 states reported offering services at age 14.[8] In addition, the funding formula is based on the total number of all children in foster care. However, some states have a larger share of youth eligible for independent living services than other states, even when their eligibility age range is the same. For example, of the 15 states reporting in our survey that youth are eligible for services between the ages of 14 and 21, 3 states had 25 percent or less of their foster care population within this age range, while in 3 other states, this age range accounted for over 40 percent of the total foster care population.[9]

States Expanded and Improved Services for Youth after FCIA, but Reported That Gaps in Critical Services Remain

In our 2004 survey, 40 states reported expanding services to youth younger than they had previously served, and 36 states reported serving older youth, but states reported service gaps in critical areas, such as mental health and housing. The number of states that reported providing core independent living services, such as independent living skills assessments, daily living skills training, and counseling to youth younger than 16 more than doubled after FCIA. Similarly, more states reported offering these supports and services to youth who were emancipated from foster care.

Many states also began to offer the new services to support youth that emancipated from foster care. These services include the Education and Training Vouchers, Medicaid health insurance, and assistance with room and board.

- *ETV:* All states, the District of Columbia, and Puerto Rico began receiving funds under the ETV program to assist youth seeking postsecondary education, but 26 states did not spend all of the funding received (see app. II). A report from the National Resource Center for Youth Development showed that states provide a range of benefits to youth eligible for ETVs.[10] Over 90 percent of 38 state independent living coordinators responding to a survey reported offering financial support to youth for room and board, school supplies, equipment and uniforms, school-related fees, and transportation costs. Eighty-four percent of states made payments for child care for the dependents of youth, and 60 percent of state reported making payments for college or university health plans on behalf of youth.[11] States were challenged to spend all of their funding allotment. Mississippi returned almost all of its 2004 ETV funds, and 14 other states returned over 20 percent of their funding allotment.[12]

- *Medicaid:* Recent information from the American Public Human Services Association shows that all states are now using or planning to use the Chafee option or other means to extend Medicaid coverage to youth. In our 2004 survey, 31 of 50 state independent living coordinators had reported offering Medicaid benefits to at least some emancipated youth to help them maintain access to health care benefits while they transitioned to independence. In 2007, the American Public Human Services Association reported that 22 states planned or have already started using the Chafee option to offer Medicaid coverage to youth who age out of foster care.[13] The study also found that the remaining 28 states and the District of Columbia were reported to be using other methods, such as the State Children's Health Insurance Program or the Medicaid waiver demonstration program, to extend coverage to youth.
- *Housing assistance:* In our 2004 survey, 46 states reported that they offered assistance with room and board to youth who had been emancipated from foster care, and the 4 states we visited reported offering a range of housing supports to assist youth. At the time of our visit, Connecticut provided several housing options to meet the needs of youth at varying levels of independence, including group homes, supervised apartment sites, and unsupervised apartment sites with periodic visits from case managers. While 3 other states we visited offered a more limited supply of housing options, all provided some type of housing subsidy or placement.
- *Existing services:* Chafee Program funds were also used to improve the quality of existing independent living services and refocus the attention of their programs, according to state officials we visited. For example, local officials in Florida said that prior to FCIA, training in daily living skills was provided haphazardly, and in many cases unqualified staff taught classes even though such training was considered a core component of their independent living program. At the time of our visit, Florida officials said that the state redesigned staff training, improved instructor quality, and was better prepared to provide youth with the skills necessary to live independently outside of the foster care system.

States differed in the proportion of eligible youth served under their respective independent living programs. In our 2004 survey, 40 states reported serving about 56,000 youth—or approximately 44 percent of youth in foster care who were eligible for independent living services in these states.14 About one-third of reporting states were serving less than half of their eligible foster care youth population, while an equal percentage of states were serving three-fourths or more. While states expanded eligibility to younger youth, most services continued to be directed at youth age 16 and older in most of the states we visited.

Certain gaps in the availability of critical services were reported, which may have contributed to the challenge of serving higher numbers of eligible youth.[15] States also reported that these challenges were more prominent in rural areas. Service gaps included the following:

- *Mental health services:* Youth in foster care often require mental health services continuing beyond emancipation. However, states continue to be challenged in providing youth with a smooth transition between the youth and adult mental health systems. Of the 4 states we visited in 2004, 3 cited difficulties due to more stringent eligibility requirements in the adult system, different levels of services, and long waiting lists for services. Challenges with mental health services remained in 2006, when 32 state child welfare directors responding to our survey reported dissatisfaction with the level of mental health services.[16]
- *Mentoring services:* Research studies indicate that the presence of positive adult role models is critical for youth in foster care because family separations and placement disruptions have been found to hinder the development of enduring bonds. Although the majority of states reported in our 2004 survey that they offered mentoring programs to youth, officials in the states we visited cited challenges in providing all youth with access to mentoring programs to establish and maintain such relationships.[17] For example, in Connecticut, one program director reported challenges recruiting adults to serve as mentors, especially men willing to make a 1-year commitment to an adolescent boy. In addition, some state and local officials and service providers seemed unclear on what should be included in a high-quality mentoring program and how to identify qualified service providers.
- *Securing safe and suitable housing:* Providing appropriate housing also remains a critical service gap. Youth we spoke with across the 4 states we visited in 2004 said that locating safe and stable housing after leaving foster care was one of their primary concerns in their transition to

independence, and state officials reported challenges meeting youths' housing needs. Youth reported difficulties renting housing because of a lack of an employment history, a credit history, or a cosigner. State and local officials in the states we visited said the availability of housing resources for foster youth during their initial transition from foster care depended on where they lived, and in some cases the benefits provided did not completely meet the needs of youth, or were available only to certain youth. For example, at the time of our visit, local officials in Washington reported that housing subsidies may not completely offset expenses for youth in expensive urban areas, like Seattle, and that rental housing in some rural areas was scarce. This service gap was identified by states again in our 2006 survey, as 31 state child welfare directors reported dissatisfaction with the level of housing for foster youth transitioning to independence.

- *Youth and foster family engagement:* State and local officials, as well as service providers in the 4 states we visited said that it was difficult to get some youth to participate in the independent living programs and that foster parents were sometimes reluctant partners. While youth were generally offered incentives, such as cash stipends, to participate in daily living skills training or other activities, officials emphasized that participation is voluntary and it is critical for foster parents to support and encourage youth participation in the program.[18]

STATES REPORTED INCREASED COORDINATION WITH FEDERAL AND STATE PROGRAMS TO PROVIDE INDEPENDENT LIVING SERVICES TO YOUTH, BUT BARRIERS HINDER LINKAGES ACROSS PROGRAMS

After FCIA, 49 states reported increased coordination with a number of federal, state, and local programs that can provide or supplement independent living services, but officials from the 4 states we visited reported several barriers in developing the linkages necessary to access services under these programs across local areas. States we surveyed reported working with a range of service provides, such as Job Corps, workforce boards, and local housing agencies.[19]

States we visited used different strategies to develop linkages among state youth programs. Three of the states we visited reported establishing state-level work groups that included representatives from the independent living program and other state agencies to bring agency officials together to discuss the needs of youth in foster care and possible strategies for improving service delivery. For example, Florida's legislature mandated a state-level work group to facilitate information sharing at the state level among various agencies, such as the State Departments of Children and Families and Education, the Agency for Workforce Innovation, and the Agency for Health Care Administration. Additional strategies states developed to establish linkages with other federal, state, or local programs included establishing liaisons between agencies or programs or through less formal collaborative arrangements. Officials also reported developing linkages with other private resources in their communities, such as business owners, to provide services to youth in the independent living program.

Despite states' efforts, we continued to find in our 2006 survey that states were least likely to address challenges in providing services such as mental health that are typically provided outside of the child welfare system by other agencies. Officials in the 4 states we visited in 2004 reported several barriers that hinder their ability to establish linkages with other agencies and programs, including the lack of information on the array of programs available in each state or local area and differences in program priorities. Officials from 3 states said that they relied on local officials to identify potential partners and initiate and maintain coordination efforts, and while individuals in some local areas may have developed successful collaborations with service providers in their area, these relationships have not always been expanded statewide. To some extent, this has been due to the fact that state and local child welfare officials differ in their awareness of resources available from other agencies. Some gaps in awareness may be partly due to turnover rates for caseworkers reported by the states we visited.[20] Caseworkers' lack of knowledge about available programs may have contributed to foster parents and youth reporting that they were unaware of the array of services available from other federal, state, or local programs. In addition, officials cited barriers to establishing linkages with other federal and state programs because of different program priorities. Differences in performance goals among programs can affect the ability of independent living staff to obtain services for foster youth from other agencies. In North Carolina, state officials we visited in 2006 said that about 70 percent of children and families in the child welfare system received services from multiple public agencies, and the Catalog of Domestic Assistance (CFDA)—a repository of information on all federal assistance programs—lists over 300 federal programs that provide youth and family services. In October 2003, the White House Task Force for Disadvantaged Youth recommended that the CFDA be modified to provide a search feature that can be used to identify locations where federally funded programs were operating.[21]

States' and HHS's Actions in Response to FCIA Requirements Have Not Yet Established Accountability for Independent Living Programs

All states developed multiyear plans as required under FCIA and submitted annual progress reports to ACF for their independent living programs, but the absence of standard comprehensive information within and across state plans and reports precludes using them at the state and federal levels to monitor how well the programs are working to serve foster care youth. HHS has not yet implemented its plan to collect information to measure states' program performance, and while some states reported collecting some data, states have experienced difficulties in contacting youth to determine their outcomes. HHS has begun to evaluate selected independent living programs.

- *State plans and annual reports:* All states developed state plans as required by FCIA that described independent living services they planned to provide to foster care youth and submitted annual reports to ACF, but for several reasons, these plans and reports cannot be used to assess states' independent living programs. While ACF officials stated that the plans and annual reports served as the primary method the agency used to monitor states' use of the Chafee Program funds, ACF did not require states to use a uniform reporting format, set specific baselines for measuring progress, or report on youths' outcomes. As a result, each state developed plans and reports that varied in their scope and level of detail, making it difficult to determine whether states had made progress in preparing foster youth to live self-sufficiently.[22]

  On the basis of our review of plans from all 50 states and the District of Columbia covering federal fiscal years 2001 through 2004, and annual reports for 45 states from federal fiscal years 2001 and 2002, we found the following:

  - Few states both organized the information in their plans to address the purposes of FCIA and presented specific strategies they would use to meet these purposes.

- The plans vary in their usefulness in establishing outcomes the states intended to achieve for youth.
- Annual reports for all 45 states contained information that did not directly relate to information in their state plan, making it unclear whether the differences were due to service changes or missing information.
- Of the 90 annual progress reports we reviewed, 52 reports did not include clear data that could be used to determine progress toward meeting the goals of the states' independent living programs.

ACF officials said that they recognize the limitations of these documents as tools to monitor states' use of independent living program funds, but explained that they rely on states' to self-certify that their independent living programs adhere to FCIA requirements. Staff in ACF's 10 regional offices conduct direct oversight of the program by reviewing the plans and reports, interpreting guidance, and communicating with the states. However, officials in three offices reported during our 2004 review that their review of the documents was cursory and that the plans and annual reports do not serve as effective monitoring tools. In addition, ACF officials reported that the Child and Family Services Review (CFSR) used to evaluate the states' overall child welfare systems could serve as a tool to monitor independent living programs, but the CFSR is limited in the type and amount of data collected on youth receiving independent living services.

- *National Youth in Transition Database:* ACF has not completed efforts to develop a plan to collect data on youths' characteristics, services, and outcomes in response to the FCIA requirement, and some states that are attempting to collect information on youths' outcomes are experiencing difficulties. In 2000, ACF started to develop the National Youth in Transition Database (NYTD) to collect information needed to effectively monitor and measure states' performance in operating independent living programs. The agency issued proposed rules on July 14, 2006, but as of July 2007, final rules governing the system have not been issued.[23]

The proposed rules include an approach to collect information on all youth who received independent living services, youth who are in foster care at age 17, and follow-up information on youth at ages 19 and 21. For any youth who receives independent living services from either the child welfare agency or another source supported by federal Chafee funds, the state must report a series of data elements, including the type of independent living services received, such as housing education or health education and risk prevention. These data are to be collected on an ongoing basis for as long as the youth receives services.

In order to develop a system to identify youth outcomes, HHS proposes establishing information on a baseline population of youth at age 17. All youth who turn 17 years old while in foster care would be surveyed on a series of outcomes, such as their current employment status. States would be required to conduct follow-up surveys with the youth at ages 19 and 21. HHS would allow the states to pull a sample from this baseline population with which to conduct these follow-up surveys. For example, California had over 7,500 youth in care in 2004 who were 17 years old. On the basis of the proposed sampling methodology, the state would be allowed to survey a minimum of 341 19-year-olds in the follow-up effort. According to results from our survey, in federal fiscal year 2003, 30 states attempted to contact youth who had been emancipated from foster care for initial information to determine their status, including education and employment outcomes. Of those states, most reported that they were unsuccessful in contacting more than half of the youth. Further, 21 states reported attempting to follow up with emancipated youth after a longer period of time had elapsed but had trouble reaching all the youth. Similarly, officials in the states we visited reported that collecting outcome data is especially challenging since there is little they can do to find youth unless the youth themselves initiate the contact. Further, some officials were concerned about the value of the outcome data since they believe that youth who are doing well are more likely to participate in the follow-up interviews, thus skewing the results. When HHS issued the proposed rule, it provided strategies states could use to conduct the follow-up component of the NYTD requirements. For example, the document recommends letting the youth know up-front that the agency will be contacting them in the future; suggests keeping a "case file" that tracks any activity, such as reasons why a letter was returned; and suggests that the agency establish a toll-free phone line.

- *Mutltistate evaluations:* At the time of our 2004 review, ACF expected to complete the evaluations of four approaches to delivering independent living services by December 2007. However, it is unclear if that deadline will be achieved at this point. As required by FCIA, these evaluations are expected to use rigorous scientific standards, such as an experimental research design that randomly assigns youth in independent living programs to different groups: one that is administered the experimental treatment and one that is not. HHS initiated this effort in 2001 with a nationwide review of potentially promising approaches to delivering independent living services. HHS contracted with a research institute to conduct a nationwide search to identify independent living programs that meet the criteria of the evaluation[24] and to conduct 5-year evaluations of the selected programs.[25] On the basis of the search and the established criteria, HHS selected four programs for the evaluation (see table 2).

In the report issued in 2004, we made recommendations to HHS (1) to make information available to states and local areas about other federal programs that may assist youth in their transition to self-sufficiency and provide guidance on how to access services under these programs and (2) to develop a standard reporting format for state plans and progress reports and implement a uniform process regional offices can use to assess states' progress in meeting the needs of youth in foster care and those recently emancipated from care. These recommendations have not been implemented.

CONCLUDING OBSERVATIONS

Preparing youth to successfully transition to independence is a daunting task that requires coordinated and continuous services across many social service systems including child welfare, health, education, and housing. The Chafee Program has provided a single funding stream that can be used to meet service needs across these social systems. However, this funding alone is not sufficient to overcome state challenges in meeting the varied service needs of emancipating youth. The child welfare system must work with housing agencies to remove barriers faced by youth with no employment history or cosigner, and with health agencies, to ensure a smooth transition between the youth and adult mental health systems. In addition, states continue to have difficulty building adequate service capacity for housing and mental health in all locales, and child welfare staff still struggle to identify the myriad of public and private sector programs that exist to assist youth. Our November 2004 report and our May 2007 testimony present recommendations we made to HHS to make information available to states and local areas about other federal programs that may assist youth in their transition to self-sufficiency.

HHS did not comment on our 2004 recommendation, but disagreed with our recent recommendation to improve awareness of and access to various social services funded by the federal government. HHS stated that the recommendation was insufficient to address the need for additional services, and incorrectly implied that local child welfare agencies were not already aware of and using such resources. We acknowledged that increasing awareness of existing federal resources is not the only action needed, but in the course of our work across the years, continue to find that caseworkers are sometimes unaware of the full array of federal resources, such as health and housing, available in their locale, or had not coordinated with other agencies to use them. We continue to support the view that federal action, such as modifying the CFDA, would allow caseworkers and others to more easily identify services and service providers funded by federal agencies in closest proximity to the youth and families they serve.

How well the Chafee Program has worked to improve outcomes for emancipated youth among states is still unknown 8 years after the passage of FCIA, and HHS has not yet implemented its information system that is intended to meet FCIA requirements for collecting and monitoring a state's performance. Given the significant variation in the number of youth served and services provided across states, an interim system for measuring state progress would seem to be warranted. However, while HHS has an oversight process to measure outcomes of state child welfare systems as a whole, this process no longer includes measures required by FCIA.

Similarly, while ACF's regional offices conduct much of the federal oversight for the Chafee Program, the oversight tools currently in place do not provide standard information needed to measure and compare performance across states. Our 2004 report included a recommendation to develop a standard reporting format for state plans and progress reports and implement a uniform process regional offices can use to assess states' progress in meeting the needs of youth in foster care and those recently emancipated from care. These recommendations have not been implemented.

HHS continues to disagree with our recommendation to develop a standard reporting format for state plans and progress reports, stating that such action would be overly prescriptive and impose an unnecessary burden on states. However, as reflected in our 2004 report, we continue to believe that strengthening the state reporting process is needed to provide some assurance of program accountability at the state and federal levels. HHS had agreed with our recommendation to establish a uniform process regional offices can use to assess states' progress and said that in 2005, ACF would develop and provide a review protocol to be used in regional office desk reviews of states' annual progress reports. However, ACF officials reported that they have not yet implemented such a review protocol.

Table 2. Programs Included in the Multisite Evaluation of Foster Youth Programs

Site	Program	Type of service	Age of focus	Number of youth (control and experimental)	Length of service provision	Key outcome of interest
Los Angeles County, California	Community College Life Skills (LST) Training	Classroom-based and experiential life skills training, teen support group, and exposure to community college opportunities	17	450	5 weeks (10 workshops)	Education, employment, housing stability, avoidance of risk behaviors
Los Angeles County, California	Early Start to Emancipation Preparation (ESTEP)	Structured tutoring and mentoring curriculum for youth 1-3 years behind grade level in reading and math skills	14-15	450	6 months of tutoring on average, mentoring continues less intensively after tutoring ends, for 3 months on average	Education, employment, and interpersonal and relationship skills
Kern County, California	Employment program	Employment skills training, job referral, and employment support provided through county Temporary Assistance to Needy Families agency	16	250	Ongoing through age 21	Employment and economic self-sufficiency
Massachusetts	Adolescent Outreach Program	Intensive, individualized life skills mentoring and casework	17	250	Mean of 1 year	Employment, housing stability, service linkages

Source: HHS.

Appendix I: Fiscal Year 2004 Chafee Foster Care Independence Program: Final Funds Allotted, Expended, and Returned to Federal Treasury, by State

State	Dollar amount allocated	Dollar amount expended	Dollar amount returned to the U.S. Treasury	Percentage of allotment returned to the U.S. Treasury
Alabama	$1,536,181	$1,536,181	$0	0%
Alaska	550,782	550,782	0	0
Arizona	1,606,959	1,606,959	0	0
Arkansas	764,776	764,776	0	0
California	26,112,429	26,112,429	0	0
Colorado	2,184,770	2,184,770	0	0
Connecticut	1,519,750	1,519,750	0	0
Delaware	500,000	500,000	0	0
District of Columbia	1,092,276	1,092,276	0	0
Florida	8,265,302	8,265,302	0	0
Georgia	3,120,798	3,120,798	0	0
Hawaii	703,523	703,523	0	0
Idaho	500,000	500,000	0	0
Illinois	6,316,656	6,316,656	0	0
Indiana	2,184,711	1,987,583	197,128	9.0
Iowa	1,336,412	1,336,412	0	0
Kansas	1,549,330	1,549,330	0	0
Kentucky	1,741,339	1,741,339	0	0
Louisiana	1,358,484	1,358,484	0	0
Maine	771,350	771,350	0	0
Maryland	3,048,143	2,635,510	412,633	13.5
Massachusetts	3,242,220	2,859,297	62,350	1.9
Michigan	5,235,404	5,235,404	0	0
Minnesota	2,063,393	2,063,393	0	0
Mississippi	758,148	758,148	0	0
Missouri	3,303,069	3,303,069	0	0
Montana	500,000	500,000	0	0
Nebraska	1,586,304	1,586,304	0	0
Nevada	500,000	498,650	1,350	0.3
New Hampshire	500,000	500,000	0	0
New Jersey	2,844,433	2,844,433	0	0
New Mexico	500,000	500,000	0	0
New York	11,588,972	11,588,972	0	0
North Carolina	2,405,731	2,249,851	155,880	6.5
North Dakota	500,000	457,425	42,575	8.5

(Continued)

State	Dollar amount allocated	Dollar amount expended	Dollar amount returned to the U.S. Treasury	Percentage of allotment returned to the U.S. Treasury
Ohio	5,310,180	5,310,180	0	0
Oklahoma	2,230,667	2,230,667	0	0
Oregon	2,216,643	2,216,643	0	0
Pennsylvania	5,341,822	5,279,535	62,287	1.2
Puerto Rico	2,124,039	2,124,039	0	0
Rhode Island	611,725	611,725	0	0
South Carolina	1,238,495	1,238,495	0	0
South Dakota	500,000	500,000	0	0
Tennessee	2,353,574	2,353,574	0	0
Texas	5,413,220	5,412,566	654	0 (0.01)
Utah	500,000	500,000	0	0
Vermont	500,000	500,000	0	0
Virginia	1,710,740	1,710,740	0	0
Washington	2,332,664	2,332,664	0	0
West Virginia	769,310	769,310	0	0
Wisconsin	1,955,276	1,955,276	0	0
Wyoming	500,000	498,996	1,004	0.2
Total	**$137,900,000** [a.]	**$136,643,566**	**$935,861**	**0% (.001%)**

Source: Subcommittee on Income Security and Family Support, Committee on Ways and Means, House of Representatives via the Congressional Research Service presentation of HHS data, July 2007.

[a]The total mandatory funds for this program are $140 million. However, the statute provides that a certain percentage of those funds be set aside for HHS to conduct (or fund) research, evaluation, and technical assistance.

Appendix II: Fiscal Year 2004 Chafee Education and Training Vouchers: Funds Allotted, Expended, and Returned to Federal Treasury, by State

State	Dollar amount allocated	Dollar amount expended	Dollar amount returned to the U.S. Treasury	Percentage of allotment returned to the U.S. Treasury
Alabama	$501,312	$501,312	$0	0%
Alaska	179,694	158,938	20,756	11.6
Arizona	524,273	524,273	0	0
Arkansas	249,575	249,575	0	0
California	8,519,233	8,452,447	66,786	0.8
Colorado	712,785	712,785	0	0
Connecticut	495,822	495,822	0	0
Delaware	73,625	73,625	0	0
District of Columbia	270,123	270,123	0	0
Florida	2,696,572	2,106,077	590,495	21.9
Georgia	1,018,431	1,018,431	0	0
Hawaii	229,526	228,762	764	0.3
Idaho	103,074	71,429	31,645	30.7
Illinois	2,060,822	2,060,822	0	0
Indiana	712,952	712,952	0	0
Iowa	436,007	436,007	0	0
Kansas	505,472	232,828	272,644	53.9
Kentucky	568,115	383,562	184,553	32.5
Louisiana	400,401	400,401	0	0
Maine	251,655	224,651	27,004	10.7
Maryland	994,722	546,876	447,846	45.0
Massachusetts	1,057,781	1,057,781	0	0
Michigan	1,708,505	841,705	866,800	50.7
Minnesota	673,186	633,908	39,278	5.7
Mississippi	247,412	1,795	245,617	99.3
Missouri	1,077,913	304,222	773,691	71.8
Montana	157,066	157,066	0	0
Nebraska	517,535	517,535	0	0
Nevada	138,764	138,764	0	0
New Hampshire	103,241	103,241	0	0
New Jersey	928,002	928,002	0	0
New Mexico	159,478	133,294	26,184	16.4
New York	3,454,364	3,317,873	136,491	4.0
North Carolina	785,079	785,079	0	0
North Dakota	100,579	44,943	55,636	55.3

(Continued)

State	Dollar amount allocated	Dollar amount expended	Dollar amount returned to the U.S. Treasury	Percentage of allotment returned to the U.S. Treasury
Ohio	1,741,616	1,282,013	459,603	26.4
Oklahoma	727,760	692,465	35,295	4.9
Oregon	723,184	424,309	298,875	41.3
Pennsylvania	1,742,780	1,640,714	102,066	5.9
Puerto Rico	693,152	497,325	195,827	28.3
Rhode Island	199,577	199,577	0	0
South Carolina	404,061	404,061	0	0
South Dakota	115,969	72,411	43,558	37.6
Tennessee	767,858	637,334	130,524	17.0
Texas	1,766,074	803,113	962,961	54.5
Utah	150,993	150,993	0	0
Vermont	120,794	120,794	0	0
Virginia	558,132	312,991	245,141	43.9
Washington	761,037	761,037	0	0
West Virginia	250,989	250,989	0	0
Wisconsin	637,913	554,677	83,236	13.1
Wyoming	87,518	87,518	0	0
Total	**$44,062,503**	**$37,719,227**	**$6,343,276**	**14.4%**

Source: Subcommittee on Income Security and Family Support, Committee on Ways and Means, House of Representatives via the Congressional Research Service presentation of HHS data, July 2007.

End Notes

[1] The Chafee Program receives funding under Title IV-E of the Social Security Act. Title IV-E authorizes the appropriation of federal funds to states for the purpose of developing and operating foster care and transitional independent living programs and providing payments to adoptive parents of eligible foster children with special needs. In 2006, the adoption program received approximately $1.8 billion, and the foster care program received approximately $4.6 billion.

[2] See GAO, *Foster Youth: HHS Actions Could Improve Coordination of Services and Monitoring of States' Independent Living Programs*, GAO-05-25 (Washington, D.C.: Nov.18, 2004).

[3] See GAO, *Child Welfare: Additional Federal Action Could Help States Address Challenges in Providing Services to Children and Families*, GAO-07-850T (Washington, D.C.: May 15, 2007).

[4] The actual amount divided among the states, the District of Columbia, and Puerto Rico totaled $137.9 million. Under the law, 1.5 percent of the $140 million is reserved for evaluation, technical assistance, performance measurement, and data collection activities conducted by HHS. States must provide matching contributions of 20 percent to receive Chafee Program funds. The matching contribution may be in cash or in-kind contributions of services, equipment, or property.

[5] A hold-harmless clause in FCIA ensures that states with smaller populations received either $500,000 or the amount of independent living funds they received in federal fiscal year 1998, whichever amount is greater.

[6] We calculated this figure using financial data from HHS on the FCIA funding allocations in federal fiscal year 2004 and Adoption and Foster Care Analysis and Reporting System (AFCARS) data from federal fiscal year 2002 because funding allocations are calculated using foster care population data from AFCARS 2 years prior to the funding year. These calculations also included states' 20 percent match requirement. However, states may use other funds to pay for services, and these calculations do not reflect any additional funding. To determine the eligible population for each state, we used the age ranges that states reported in our 2004 survey and AFCARS data on the numbers of youth in each age group. For example, Alabama reported in our survey serving youth between 14 and 21 with independent living services. According to data the state reported to AFCARS, 2,081 youth in this age range were in care in Alabama in federal fiscal year 2002. However, this calculation excludes youth emancipated from foster care, since AFCARS does not capture this information.

[7] Nationwide, the average funding for independent living services available per eligible youth in foster care was about $1,090 in federal fiscal year 2004.

[8] According to results from our 2004 survey, 4 states began services at age 12, 7 states began services at age 13, 27 states began services at age 14, 9 states began services at age 15, and 4 states began services at age 16.

[9] These calculations are based on AFCARS data, which do not include emancipated youth.

[10] See Michelle L. Kessler, *Educating Youth in Care: The First Year of Education and Training Vouchers* (Tulsa, Oklahoma: 2004).

[11] Of the 38 responding states, 54 percent also indicated that they pay for other tangible benefits such as tutoring, Internet access, computers, books, medications required to allow youth to be successful with their studies, payment for housing over the holidays and vacations when dorms are closed, preparatory tests, and study materials.

[12] Overall, more than 14 percent of 2004 ETV funding was returned to the U.S. Treasury. As states have 2 years to spend these funds, information on later years is not currently available.

[13] Arizona, California, Florida, Indiana, Iowa, Kansas, Massachusetts, Mississippi, Nevada, New Jersey, Oklahoma, Rhode Island, South Carolina, South Dakota, Texas, Utah, and Wyoming reported enacting the Chafee Medicaid option. Maryland, Missouri, New Mexico, North Carolina, and Wisconsin reported planning to pursue the use of the Chafee Medicaid option. See American Public Human Services Association, *Medicaid Access for Youth Aging Out of Foster Care* (Washington, D.C.: 2007).

[14] We were unable to identify comparable data on the proportion of eligible youth in foster care that received independent living services prior to the passage of FCIA.

[15] State and local administrators reported some similar gaps in our 1999 report. They noted that their independent living programs fell short in key areas, including gaps in employment, daily living skills, and housing services. See GAO, *Foster Care: Effectiveness of Independent Living Services Unknown,* HEHS-00-13 (Washington, D.C.: Nov. 5, 1999).

[16] Child welfare directors in many states were also dissatisfied with the level of substance abuse services (31) and dental care services (29). Dissatisfaction with physical health services and access to Medicaid was cited by 10 states.

[17] Forty-five states reported having mentoring services for youth in foster care, and 39 states reported having mentoring services for emancipated youth.

[18] The National Resource Center for Youth Services—under contract with HHS—reported in 2004 on a study conducted by the Casey Family Services, which found that not all young adults accepted supports extended to them. In a sample of 115 alumni of foster care, only 41 percent incurred expenses for services after age 19. Some youth are simply ready to end their relationship with the child welfare system when they are legally able. Others, however, may not incur expenses for services because they are not aware of the benefits that are available. See Kessler, *Educating Youth in Care.*

[19] Job Corps is an education and vocational training program administered by the U.S. Department of Labor to service youth ages 16 through 24 years. The Workforce Investment Act established workforce investment boards. Each state workforce investment board is responsible for developing statewide workforce policies and overseeing its local workforce investment boards. The local workforce investment boards, in turn, are responsible for developing local workforce policies and overseeing operations.

[20] See also GAO, *Child Welfare: HHS Could Play a Greater Role in Helping Child Welfare Agencies Recruit and Retain Staff*, GAO-03-357 (Washington, D.C.: Mar. 31, 2003).

[21] A similar model may be found on an HHS Web link, http://ask.hrsa.gov/pc/, where users can enter a ZIP code to find the closest community health center locations offering medical, mental, dental, and other health services on a sliding fee scale.

[22] We previously reported similar problems using state reports for federal monitoring of independent living programs prior to FCIA and had recommended that HHS establish a uniform set of data elements and a standard reporting format for state reporting on independent living programs. See GAO-HEHS-00-13.

[23] Chafee National Youth in Transition Database, 71 Fed. Reg. 40,346 (July 14, 2006) (to be codified at 45 C.F.R. pt. 1356).

[24] In the nationwide search, HHS contractors sought programs that met four criteria for a rigorous research study: Programs should be directed, at least in part, at youth leaving foster care or expected to remain in foster care until adulthood; be innovative, of national significance, and capable of expanding into new geographic areas; be willing and capable of participating in experiments involving random assignment of youth to treatment services or the alternative services; and have an adequate sample size and should have a need for the services greater than what is currently available so an experiment would not reduce the total number of youth serviced by the program. Many programs could not support a randomized study because their youth population was not large enough to ensure youth did not go without services.

[25] HHS contracted with the Urban Institute and its partners—the Chapin Hall Center for Children and the National Opinion Research Center.

In: Foster Care and African-American Youth
Editor: Joanna Kaczmarek
ISBN: 978-1-60741-541-1

Chapter 4

HEARING ON RACIAL DISPROPORTIONALITY IN FOSTER CARE, UNITED STATES HOUSE OF REPRESENTATIVES, SUBCOMMITTEE ON INCOME SECURITY AND FAMILY SUPPORT*

Child Welfare League of America

The Child Welfare League of America represents hundreds of state and local child welfare organizations including both public and private, and faith-based agencies. CWLA members provide a range of child welfare services from prevention to placement services including adoptions, foster care, kinship placements, and services provided in a residential setting. CWLA's vision is that every child will grow up in a safe, loving, and stable family and that we will lead the nation in building public will to realize this vision.

* This is an edited, reformatted and augmented version of a Child Welfare League of America publication dated July 2008.

THE OVERREPRESENTATION OF RACIAL AND ETHNIC MINORITIES IN CHILD WELFARE

The members of this Subcommittee are well versed on the statistics, 506,000[1] children in foster care placements at the end of the federal fiscal year 2005, and 800,000[2] children spend at least some time in foster care each year. In addition in 2005 there were 3.3 million reports of abuse and neglect which resulted in 899,000 children substantiated as abused or neglected in that same year. For reasons we will outline it is important to note that approximately 40 percent of those children did not receive follow up services[3]. In another part of the child welfare system, which is often overlooked, more than 24,000 youth leave foster care simply because they become too "old" or "aged-out" of the system.[4]

Children of color, belonging to various cultural, ethnic, and racial communities (primarily African American, Latino/Hispanic, and Native/Indigenous American) are disproportionately represented in the child welfare system and frequently experience disparate and inequitable service provision. The overrepresentation of children of color in child welfare and other social service systems (e.g., juvenile justice) is linked to social, class and economic factors that must be addressed to ensure that the needs of all children are fairly and appropriately served. Federal, state, and local governments; the child welfare system; and the communities they serve must ensure that all children, regardless of their cultural, ethnic, or racial identity, receive services that address the full spectrum of their needs in a manner that reflects the cultural strengths of their families.

As the GAO and others have determined, while African American children made up less than 15 percent of the overall child population based on 2000 census data, they represented 27 percent of the children who entered foster care in 2004. The GAO also found that in that same year African American children represented 34 percent of the children remaining in care at year's end.[5]

RESEARCH CITES POVERTY AS A CONTRIBUTING FACTOR TO DISPROPORTIONALITY

The GAO report found that 23% of African Americans lived below poverty levels compared to only 6% of white children.[6] The rate of single-parent families, an issue also related to poverty, is higher for African American families. The challenge of poverty is important in addressing this issue because families in poverty have difficulty accessing needed services, which support families and prevent incidents of neglect or conditions that can add to the stress of parenting. Lack of access to services hinders the ability of parents to complete required services if a child is removed.

In some instances affordable and adequate housing, substance abuse treatment, mental health services and family services such as parenting classes, home visiting and counseling are critical to family reunification. A service in short supply or not available creates a barrier to both prevention of abuse and reunification when a child has been removed.

POINTS OF ENTRY

Key to understanding this issue is to not overlook another important finding GAO and others have offered, that African American children not only were more likely to be placed in out of home care but with each decision point in the child welfare process the disproportionality or over representation grows. In some areas of the country depending on the population and community this overrepresentation is found among Native American children and Hispanic populations.

Frequently the first point of access to services can be the Child Protective Services (CPS) system. As we have already referenced annual data indicates that of the approximate 900,000 substantiated as abuse and or neglected, 40 percent do not receive follow up services.[7] There can be a variety of reasons for this annually consistent number including the way data is collected to refusal to participant in follow up services but the fact that such a high percentage do not receive services indicates that a significant number of families do not have access to supports that could prevent more serious incidents of abuse and neglect.

A recent analysis by the Congressional Research Services (CRS) conducted at the request of the Chairman of this Committee, Representative Charles Rangel, determined that overrepresentation of children of color was found at several points of the child welfare system starting from the investigation or entry point CRS[8] noted:

> "...at least one large five-state study has shown that the race/ethnicity of victims is largely in proportion to the population of children investigated. This suggests that the community of reporters, (e.g., family, friends, and neighbors, and social service, medical and school personnel) tends to over-report Black children but that once the decision to investigate is made, race/ethnicity is not an

important factor in the determination of maltreatment. Nonetheless, because Black children are over-represented in the population of children investigated, a proportionate victim determination means Black children will make up a larger share of child maltreatment victims than their share of the general child population."

In examining other factors such as age and poverty CRS wrote:

"Separate analysis of National Child Abuse and Neglect Data System data that looked at race/ethnicity, area poverty rate, and age in relation to removals, found that the risk of removal was highest for all income groups and race/ethnicities for children under age one. At the same time, Black infants living in counties with high poverty rates had a removal rate of 50 per 1000 black children in the population. This appears to leave them extraordinarily vulnerable compared to their Hispanic and White counterparts who had removal rates of 13 and 10 per 1000 children of their respective race/ethnic groups.[9]

REUNIFICATION

The same barriers and problems at the entry point can exist at the exit point as well. In recent years we have made progress in reducing the number of children in out of home care. Nationally the number of children in care has been reduced from 562,712 in 1999 to 509,483 in 2005.[10] Despite this decline, barriers to permanency remain and can be quite extensive. Reunification is the first permanency option states consider for children entering care. Yet, in many ways, it is the most challenging option to achieve. We know that of the 280,660 children exiting out-of-home care in 2005, sixty-four percent were reunited with their parents or other family members. Research of national data indicates that White children were almost four times more likely to be reunified with their families than Black children.[11] For single-parent households, reunification of Black children with their families is less likely than for White and Hispanic children and their families.[12]

An examination of the data on the length of stay while in foster care also reflects on the challenges. On September 30, 2004 there were 509,662 children in out-of-home care. Of these children approximately 34 percent were African American and 40 percent were White. Overall, children were in care for an average of 30 months with a median of 17 months. African American children were in foster care significantly longer than children of other races. Both the mean and the median for time spent in care were higher for ethnic and racial minorities.

While White children spent, on average about two years in foster care it was significantly higher for other populations. (Table below)[13]

Length of Time in Out-Of-Home-Care, 2004

Race/Ethnicity of Children in Care	Mean (months)	Median (months)
African American	39.4	22.8
American Indian/Alaskan Native	26.1	15.0
Asian	26.0	15.2
Hispanic	28.7	16.4
Native Hawaiian/Pacific Islander	21.9	14.0
White	23.5	13.6
Two or More Races	23.4	14.6

ADOPTION

One area that has received special focus in regard to overrepresentation is the field of adoptions from the foster care system. Since the 1970s, the number of White infants available for adoption has sharply declined in the U.S. Although U.S. agencies continue to provide adoption services for infants generally, this group now constitutes a small part of the population of children in need of adoption planning and services.

By contrast, the number of children in the nation's out-of-home care placements who need adoption has grown significantly. As a result of a range of social conditions and policy changes, an increasing proportion of children in care have the goal of adoption. In 2005 122,195 children in care were waiting to be adopted, meaning parental rights had been terminated or other steps were taken, following state policy or law, to move the child toward adoption.[14] These children may have a range of challenging needs, including prenatal exposure to alcohol and other drugs, medical fragility, a history of physical or sexual abuse, or membership in a sibling group. Thousands of older children, for whom agencies traditionally have had difficulty finding placements, also await adoptive families. Although Black children exited care via adoption in higher numbers than other ethnic groups, adoption finalizations for children still take longer than for white children[15]

A recent report from the Evan B. Donaldson Adoption Institute evaluated the impact of legislation aimed at addressing the over-representation of minority children in the population of children awaiting adoption. The Multi-Ethnic

Placement Act (MEPA) of 1994 was enacted to ensure that race was not a barrier to the timely adoption of children whose parental rights had been terminated. The conclusion drawn was that MEPA "has not removed barriers to permanency for African American children". The Donaldson report noted that between FY 1998 and FY 2005, there was only a slight decline in the amount of time minority children awaited adoption from 45 months to 42 months.[16] The 2007 GAO report similarly found that minorities continue to be in foster care longer than Caucasian children by 9 months.[17]

PERMANENCY THROUGH KINSHIP CARE

Research demonstrates the importance of children being nurtured in a stable family environment, confirming the need to move those who must enter foster care into permanent living situations as quickly as possible. Recent studies suggest that, when children must leave their families, well-supported kinship placements have the potential to provide more stable and normalizing environments than unrelated family care.[18]

Kinship care is a situation in which an adult family member, such as a grandparent, aunt, uncle, or other relative, provides a caring home for a child who is not able to live with his or her parents. The practice is not new, but it is growing partly because repeated studies and CWLA Best Practice Guidelines have revealed the value of placing children with a relative when appropriate. The financial difficulties many relatives experience potentially threaten the use and merit of this practice, however.

Subsidized guardianship is another important permanency option for relatives who care for children. In 2005, the U.S. Department of Health and Human Services (HHS) released findings and evaluations of the seven state waiver demonstration programs that allow federal Title IV-E Foster Care and Adoption Assistance funding to support guardianship programs. These findings reflect that non-relative guardianship is a viable and effective option for child welfare workers to consider. The major findings include: the availability of assisted guardianship as a permanency option may decrease the length of out-of-home placements; combined data from two states reveals that less than 5% of the children in guardianship placements return to foster care; children in guardianship placements fare as well as those in other permanency settings on several measures of well-being, including school performance, engagement in risky behaviors, and access to community resources; and the use of guardianship placements shows statistically significant signs of positive outcomes, with more exits from foster care resulting in reunification or adoption.

The GAO report we have cited here also recognizes the important and significant role that the use of kinship care can have in moving children in to a permanent family arrangement.

Recent new research presented here in Washington this past June examined children from three groups, those who remained in foster care, those who entered kinship care at the outset of a placement and those that went from foster care to kinship care at a later period. The study, "Impact of Kinship Care on Behavioral Well-being for Children in Out-of-Home Care," showed that children in kinship care had fewer behavioral problems 3 years after placement than those children in foster care after an equal time frame.[19]

YOUTH LEAVING FOSTER CARE

In 2005 over 24,000[20] young people exited the foster care system due to age, a number that appears to be increasing. Young people transitioning out of foster care are significantly impacted by the instability that accompanies long periods of out of home placement. Youth in the foster care system are often confronted with emotional, behavioral, developmental, and health challenges. The life events of these young people place them at an increased risk for experiencing adversity. In the midst of elevated rates of homelessness, poor educational outcomes, low wages, unemployment, long-term dependency on public assistance, incarceration and health issues, young people "aging out" of the foster care system are also experiencing pregnancies and early parenthood. Confronting and overcoming these challenges is more difficult without support networks or familial connections and impedes their transition into adulthood.

The nation's child welfare system is starting the implementation stages of collecting more accurate information on the fate of young people who leave the foster care system as a result of becoming too old. We do know that a disproportionate percentage of children waiting to be adopted are ethnic and racial minorities. We also know that over 21 percent of foster children are sixteen or older and that a disproportionate percentage are ethnic and racial minorities. So we can draw broad conclusions in regard to young people aging out and the overrepresentation of racial and ethnic minorities in this part of the child welfare population.

TRIBAL POPULATIONS

In 1978, Congress passed the Indian Child Welfare Act (ICWA, P.L. 95-608) to preserve cultural and family ties among Native American children and families and to ensure respect for tribal authority in decisions concerning the placement of Indian children in out-of-home care. ICWA requires that states identify Indian children and notify the child's parents and tribe of their rights to intervene in a custody proceeding. ICWA also requires certain procedures regarding the use of tribal courts, child custody proceedings, tribal intervention standards, and placement preferences. The act establishes requirements for states before they remove an Indian child, which involves efforts to prevent the breakup of the Indian family, and standards for court findings.

Studies preceding the passage of ICWA showed that between 1969 and 1974, 25% to 35% of all Native American children in some states were removed from their homes and placed in foster care or adoptive homes. In certain states, Native American children were 13 times more likely to be removed from their families than were non-Indian children.[21]

In 2005, Congress directed the GAO to study the impact of ICWA to determine if the ICWA requirements were causing delays in the placement of Native American children. The GAO concluded that it did not result in poorer outcomes for children. Those states that could provide data showed that there was no clear link or evidence ICWA was harmful in its impact. Interviews with tribes and states that participated in the study indicated that the law facilitated the availability of greater resources and cooperation between tribes and states in providing services to and protection of Indian children.[22]

The GAO proposed that HHS review information made available by states through their Child and Family Service Reviews (CFSRs). This review found that 10 of 51 state reports did not mention ICWA implementation. GAO also proposed that states be required to include in their annual progress and services reports any significant ICWA issues not addressed in the Program Improvement Plans (PIPs) that resulted from the CFSRs. One of the key findings of the GAO study was the problem of measuring ICWA compliance and assisting improved compliance when there was no explicitly named oversight agency.

In addition to these overall challenges is the reality that most federal funds that could address the needs of children from tribes that come into contact with the child welfare system are not provided directly to tribal governments. This is especially significant in regard to Title IV-E foster care and adoption assistance, the two biggest sources of funding.

LEGISLATIVE RECOMMENDATIONS

CWLA is especially pleased that this Subcommittee has taken the initiative and provided the leadership in taking a first but significant step in addressing some of these challenges with its drafting and passage of the Fostering Connection to Success Act (H.R. 6307.) In particular we appreciate the efforts of Chairman McDermott and Ranking Member Weller. This bipartisan legislation takes some critical steps by extending Title IV-E funds to kinship placements and to tribal governments. In addition the legislation would provide extended services to foster youth who are forced out of the system at an age before they are fully prepared to live independently. The bill also takes the important step of extending the adoption incentives program with an added focus on those older children who remain in the system waiting to be adopted. There are also several other provision which can help address some of the challenges that contribute to the overrepresentation in child welfare. We should not overlook the impact that adequate training for caseworkers, and access to important basic needs for children in care including education and health care can have on these challenges.

Once again CWLA commends the leadership of this Subcommittee and the House for crafting and passing a bill that is significant, bipartisan, and is paid for. We are encouraged by the scheduled action by the Senate Finance Committee to address their version of this legislation in the next few days. We hope that in the remaining weeks of this Congress agreement can be reached on this legislation.

In the next Congress we hope members will examine other areas of need. We need to look at ways that the entry points of the system can be improved upon. There are some innovations in the way some child welfare agencies are redesigning their protective services systems including the use of differential response. We also need to look at family group decision making and other approaches that seek to involve families and communities in some of these child welfare cases.

There is a great need to expand prevention, although it is challenging to define. One promising approach is home visitation programs. Congress must also look to ways to build and improve on the child welfare workforce. Again, Representative Weller and other members of the Subcommittee have assisted in this area by advancing H.R. 6307, which expands access to caseworker training, and it appears that Congress is about to allow loan forgiveness for some social workers—both needed improvements.

CWLA also hopes that members will examine ways we can increase adoptions in the foster care system, not just to address the increasing number of older children now waiting to be adopted but also to examine ways to increase the recruitment of minority adoptive parents, and to strengthen training in this area and to re-examine the Multi- Ethnic Placement Act (MEPA) and its impact in this area.

CONCLUSION

We hope Congress will complete the action that members of this Subcommittee and the House have initiated. In addition to legislation there are other avenues that must be pursued. The following major areas require further review, analysis, and action by public and private child welfare and social service administrators, staff, researchers, advocates, youth, families, and their communities. Specifically all parties need to:

Examine the rates at which children of various ethnic groups are reported and/or substantiated as abused or neglected, and the types of maltreatment that are reported and/or substantiated for these groups;
Examine the relationship between poverty, culture, individual racism, and institutional racism (within the system and in society as a whole);
Addess the lack of resources, protective factors, and community-based supports as contributing factors;
Review the decision making process, beginning with case referral and intake, and its effects on children of color and their families;
Examine the path through the service system children of color follow;
Take action to assure the availability and equitable provision of family preservation and support services;
Examine the rate of placement of children of all cultural, racial, and ethnic communities in foster and formal kinship arrangements;
Address the manner in and rate at which children of color exit the system; and
Provide special focus on the overrepresentation of children and families of color at all stages of the child welfare process.

End Notes

[1] Child Welfare League of America. (2007). *Special tabulation of the Adoption and Foster Care Analysis Reporting System*. Washington, DC: Author. back

[2] Administration on Children, Youth, and Families (ACYF). (2008).*Trends in foster care and adoption.* Washington, DC: Avaialble online at: http://www.acf.hhs.gov/programs/cb/stats research/afcars/trends.htm

[3] Administration on Children, Youth, and Families (ACYF). (2008). *Child maltreatment 2006,* Washington, DC: U.S. Department of Health and Human Services (HHS).

[4] Children who aged out of foster care are captured by the AFCARS emancipation data element. Children who exit care to emancipation are those who reached the age of majority; CWLA, Special tabulation from AFCARS. back

[5] U.S. Government Accountability Office (GAO). (2007). *African-American Children in Foster Care: Additional HHS assistance needed to help states reduce the proportion in care.* (GAO-07-816). Available online at www.gao.gov.

[6] Ibid.

[7] Administration Child Welfare League of America. (2007). *Special tabulation of the Adoption and Foster Care Analysis Reporting System.* Washington, DC: Author. back

[8] Emilie Stoltzfus. (2005).*Race/Ethnicity in child welfare* Congressional Research Service (CRS).. Washington, DC: . Available online at: http://www.cwla.org/programs/ culture

[9] Ibid.

[10] Child Welfare League of America (CWLA). (2006). Special tabulation of the Adoption and Foster Care Analysis Reporting System (AFCARS). Washington, DC: Author.

[11] Hill, R. B. (2001). The role of race in foster care placements. Paper presented at the Race Matters Forum, Chevy Chase, MD. Hill, B. (2005). http://www.racemattersconsortium.org/docs/BobHillPaper FINAL.pdf)

[12] Harris, M. & Courtney, M. (2002). The Interaction of Race, Ethnicity, and Family Structure with Respect to Timing of Family Reunification. Paper presented at the Research Roundtable On Children of Color in Child Welfare. Washington, DC: Author.

[13] Child Welfare League of America (CWLA). (2006). Special tabulation of the Adoption and Foster Care Analysis Reporting System (AFCARS). Washington, DC: Author. back.

[14] Administration Child Welfare League of America. (2007). *Special tabulation of the Adoption and Foster Care Analysis Reporting System.* Washington, DC: Author. back

[15] Barth, R. (1997). Barth, R., Courtney, M., & Berry, (1994). McRoy, Ogelsby, & Grape, (1997) as cited in Hill, 2006)

[16] Evan B. Donaldson Adoption Institute *Finding Families for African American Children: The Role of Race & Law in Foster care Adoption* (2008): Evan B. Donaldson Institute. Avaialble online at: http://www.cwla.org/advocacy

[17] U.S. Government Accountability Office (GAO). (2007). *African-American Children in Foster Care: Additional HHS assistance needed to help states reduce the proportion in care.* (GAO-07-816). Available online at www.gao.gov.

[18] Webster, D., Barth, R.P. & Needell, B. (2000). Placement stability for children in out-of home care. *Child Welfare*, 79(5), 614-631. 28 U.S. Department of Health and Human Services, Administration on Children, Youth, and Families, & Children's Bureau (2005). *Synthesis of findings: Assisted guardianship child welfare demonstrations.* Available online at http://www.acf.hhs.gov/programs/cb/programs fund/cwwaiver/agissue/. Washington, DC:

[19] Rubin, D.,Downes,K.,O'Reilly,A.,Mekonnen, R., Luan, X., Localio, R.(June 2008). *Impact of kinshipc care on behavioral well-being for Children in Out-of-home care*: Archives Pediatric Adolescent Medicine. Vol. 162., No. 6.

[20] Children who aged out of foster care are captured by the AFCARS emancipation data element. Children who exit care to emancipation are those who reached the age of majority; CWLA, Special tabulation from AFCARS. back

[21] Brown, E., Limb, G., Chance, T., & Munoz, R. (2002). *The Indian Child Welfare Act: An examination of state compliance in Arizona.* Available online at www.casey.org/Resources/Publications/NICWAComplianceInArizona.htm. Seattle, WA: Casey Family Programs; and Portland, OR: National Indian Child Welfare Association.

[22] Government Accountability Office. (2005). *Indian Child Welfare Act: Existing information on implementation issues could be used to target guidance and assistance to states.* (GAO-05-290). Washington DC: Author.

In: Foster Care and African-American Youth ISBN: 978-1-60741-541-1
Editor: Joanna Kaczmarek

Chapter 5

STATEMENT OF DARYLE CONQUERING BEAR, FORMER FOSTER YOUTH, COLORADO BEFORE THE SUBCOMMITTEE ON INCOME SECURITY AND FAMILY SUPPORT OF THE HOUSE COMMITTEE ON WAYS AND MEANS: HEARING ON RACIAL DISPROPORTIONALITY IN FOSTER CARE

Chairman McDermott, Representative Weller, and Members of the Subcommittee, thank you for inviting me to testify today. I thank the Members of the Subcommittee for their commitment to creating a better life and a brighter future for the half a million children who are living in foster care today.

At age 13, I was removed from my family and my Lakota Sioux tribe, and I was placed in foster care in Colorado. Five years later, at age 18, I "aged out" completely on my own. During the five years I spent in foster care, I lost touch with my siblings, became disconnected from my tribal customs and drifted from placement to placement. I moved four times during the five years I was in foster care, living in two group homes and two foster homes. Adjusting to different schools and rules each time I moved made it hard to stay connected to both my heritage and my family. I was separated from my grandmother, the one person that connected me with my culture and my heritage. I missed so many important moments — my sister's birthday, my brother's high school graduation, and holiday celebrations.

Traditionally, American Indian families are very close. Before I entered foster care, my youngest sister was my best friend and, as the oldest brother, my role would be to pass along knowledge to all my younger siblings. In foster care, however, I was separated from my brothers and sisters. At first, we saw one another every week and tried to stay in touch as much as we could. But then my brothers and sisters were moved to another town, and I didn't see them for over a year. One brother ran away from his group home and was sent to a placement far away. After the age of 13, I had no opportunity to be either the older brother or the tribal member I dreamed of becoming.

Being separated from your family is unbelievably hard for anyone. It is particularly hard for a child or teenager. But when you are separated from your family and isolated from your traditions and heritage, it is even more difficult. Foster care took both my family and my culture away. When I was young, I looked forward to the day I could participate in pow wows and sweat lodges — rites of passage that, in my culture, would mean I was becoming an adult. In foster care, I wasn't able to take part in those cultural events that meant so much to me. As a result, I often feel like an outsider in my own Lakota Sioux tribe in Colorado. My experience is not, unfortunately, uncommon. Many other American Indian children have similar stories to tell.

I am convinced one reason I lost connection with both my culture and my family is that most tribes cannot access federal child welfare funding to help them serve the children and families in their care. More than 560 federally recognized tribes are struggling to meet the needs of their members, but current federal law does not allow tribes to receive the direct Title IV-E funding that would help pay for these services. Only those tribes that have developed special contracts with their states can be reimbursed for providing supports and services to children and families.

This inability to directly access federal foster care funds limits tribes' capacity to meet the needs of children and families in crisis. As a result, tribes are only able to provide services for 30 to 40 percent of Native American children in foster care, and there is little or no capacity for tribes to engage in efforts to help children and families remain safely together. Tribal children often must go into the care of state agencies, reducing the chance that they and their families will receive services that are specifically geared to their culture and community.

Thanks to the leadership of this committee, especially Chairman McDermott and Representative Weller, earlier this summer the House unanimously passed the Fostering Connections to Success Act (H.R. 6307). Among its many important provisions, this bill addresses one of biggest barriers facing tribes and their ability to serve abused and neglected tribal youth. The bill would allow tribes to receive direct federal foster care funding, so that more American Indian families could remain intact and children would be able to stay strongly connected to two things that define them—their family and their culture. Many experts agree on this policy, including the national, nonpartisan Pew Commission on Children in Foster Care. The Pew Commission studied the nation's foster care system and recommended that Indian tribes have the option to directly access funding for Title IV-E.

A recent report, released jointly by Pew and National Indian Child Welfare Association, finds that American Indian and Alaskan Native children are overrepresented in foster care at more than 1.6 times the expected level. It shows that American Indian and Alaskan Native children are less likely than other children in foster care to have experienced abuse, but more likely to have experienced neglect. States with the greatest overrepresentation of Native American children in foster care include Alaska, Minnesota, Montana, Nebraska, North Dakota, Oregon, South Dakota, Utah, and Washington. **Native American children make up from one-fourth to over one-half of the foster care population in South Dakota, Alaska, Montana, and North Dakota.**

My experiences in foster care have taught me how important tradition, cultural heritage, and family are. Today I am voicing the hopes of American Indian and Alaskan Native young people across the country who are currently or have formerly been in foster care. My name is Daryle Conquering Bear, and I waiting to reconnect with my grandmother, who I lost touch with as a result of my leaving the community of the Lakota Sioux tribe when I was placed in foster care. We ask you very simply to make certain that other children don't have to endure the unnecessary losses so many of us have experienced.

Right now as you listen to my story, there are more stories taking shape – stories of native children being removed from their homes and being placed with strangers, losing their brothers and sisters, but more importantly, losing who they are as individuals, losing their culture. We hope that Congress will change child welfare legislation to give tribes the ability to serve their children and families with culturally appropriate care and understanding. American Indian and Alaskan Native kids and families have waited long enough. The time for real, lasting and meaningful reform is now. Thank you.

In: Foster Care and African-American Youth
Editor: Joanna Kaczmarek
ISBN: 978-1-60741-541-1

Chapter 6

TESTIMONY OF CASEY FAMILY PROGRAMS, HEARING ON RACIAL DISPROPORTIONALITY IN FOSTER CARE, BEFORE THE SUBCOMMITTEE ON INCOME SECURITY AND FAMILY SUPPORT, U.S. HOUSE OF REPRESENTATIVES

Oronde Miller

Good morning Mr. Chairman and members of the Subcommittee. I am Oronde Miller, Senior Director of Systems Improvement at Casey Family Programs. Casey Family Programs thanks you for the invitation to testify today before the Subcommittee on Income Security and Family Supports about promising state and community based programs and policies to address racial disproportionality in child welfare. We thank you for your continued commitment to address the issue of racial disparities. It is a challenging issue, but one that must be addressed.

Casey Family Programs is the nation's largest operating foundation focused solely on providing, improving and ultimately preventing the need for foster care. The foundation draws on over 40 years of experience and expert research and analysis to improve the lives of children and youth in foster care in two important ways: by providing direct services and supports to children and families involved in foster care, and by promoting improvements in child welfare practice and policy. In 2005 Casey began a 15-year strategic vision that we call our 2020 Strategy for Children.

As a nation, we need to take action to better care for our vulnerable children. If nothing changes in the United States between 2005 and 2020:

22,500 children will die from child abuse and neglect.

Nearly 14 million children will be confirmed as victims of abuse or neglect. 9 million more children will experience foster care.

300,000 youth will age out of foster care, most with inadequate supports to build successful adult lives.

Most of these children are children of color.

Our 2020 Strategy calls for a comprehensive change of foster care and the child welfare system. Casey's 2020 Strategy seeks to safely reduce the number of children in foster care by 50 percent by the year 2020 and reinvest savings to improve the well being of children and their families, especially in the areas of education, employment, and mental health.

As part of our strategic efforts, we are investing two billion dollars of our own endowment to improve outcomes for children who are at risk or are already involved in the child welfare system. We are partnering with states, tribes and local communities to provide technical assistance and share promising approaches to help them address many of the challenges that plague child welfare systems. We recognize that in order to reach our 2020 goals for children and families, strategies to address issues of racial disparities must be integrated into all efforts to reform the current child welfare system. Some of our work directly addresses racial disproportionality. For instance, Casey Family Programs, in collaboration with the Annie E. Casey Foundation, Casey Family Services, and the Center for Community Partnerships in Child Welfare, sponsored a Breakthrough Series Collaborative (BSC) on "Reducing Disproportionality and Disparate Outcomes for Children and Families of Color in the Child Welfare System" to help jurisdictions identify key components of change to reduce and ultimately eliminate these disparities. In addition, we have partnered with states and counties including the Texas Child Protective Services (CPS) system to address systemic factors and identify and implement practice improvements that can address the disproportional representation and disparate outcomes of children of color and their families. Casey Family Programs also is proud to be part of the Casey/CSSP Alliance on Racial Equity in Child Welfare (Alliance). One critical element of the Alliance's work is to identify locations or sites across the country, where work is being done to promote racial equity and improve outcomes for children of color in child welfare.

Some of the work we do is designed to reform child welfare more generally but has a particularly significant impact on children of color. We believe that both types of activities are necessary if we are to effectively address racial disparities in child welfare. Efforts to address racial disproportionality within states and local jurisdictions also often take this dual approach. Targeted acts to address cultural and racial bias must be accompanied by more global efforts to address the needs of all children in care or who are at risk of coming into care.

Through our work with the BSC sites, our partnerships with states and communities throughout the country and our efforts as part of the Alliance, Casey Family Programs has identified several promising and effective practices and policies to address racial disproportionality. As I highlight the initiatives in Texas and other jurisdictions, I will describe some of the policies that enabled them to intentionally address racial disproportionality. My remarks will conclude by noting what changes in federal policy can help more states to engage in effective and promising approaches.

THE TEXAS APPROACH AND EXPERIENCE

A number of states have begun to identify and address racial disproportionality and disparate outcomes for children and families of color. In fact a number of these states are represented on this panel today. Texas is one state that has been particularly comprehensive and innovative in their scope of work.

Casey Family Programs has worked in Texas for a number of years, providing direct services to many children in foster care, supporting families and communities involved in the child welfare system, and providing strategic consulting to improve the state's child welfare system. A large focus of this relationship has been to reduce racial disproportionality and disparate outcomes for children and families of color involved with Texas' foster care system as part of our overarching goal of improving the child welfare system for all children.

The Texas experience illustrates six core elements of a successful effort to address racial disproportionality in child welfare:

1) **Building Political Will to Reform the Child Welfare System Overall with a Focus on Prevention and Early Intervention** – Understanding

and addressing racial disproportionality and disparate outcomes formally became a central component of the Texas child welfare system reform efforts in 2005, although the work to make this happen began much earlier. It is important to point out the policy and political context in which these changes occurred. After a number of tragic child welfare cases, the child welfare agency, state legislature and Governor committed to improving the entire child protective services system with both improved policies that focused on prevention and a substantial increase in resources. The redesign added significant resources which reflected a strong political commitment to improving safety for all children and increased supports for relative caregivers. These additional resources and the following programmatic initiatives have produced significant results. For the first time in seven years, the number of children entering foster care in Texas decreased. Although there was a reduction in the total number of children entering care, the impact was greater in the jurisdictions where the state had focused its disproportionality efforts, particularly in the areas where they targeted community engagement.

2) **Data Driven Planning** – This political climate created an opportunity for child welfare agencies to talk about disproportionality. They were able to include this issue as part of the larger discussion on child welfare reform because they had begun collecting and analyzing data about disproportionality in child welfare years before the reform efforts began. Their research found that, even after controlling for factors such as poverty, children of color were more likely to enter care and fare worse once in care. The data was incontrovertible: patterns of poor outcomes for children of color in the Texas child welfare system was a result of historic patterns of inequity and racism that disadvantaged children, families and communities of color. Armed with this information and with the support and leadership of the executive and legislative branch, child welfare officials committed to make a cultural shift within the state child protective services system. Strategies to address racial disproportionality and disparate outcomes must begin with an analysis of data, specifically disaggregated by race and ethnicity at each of the critical decision points in a child and family's involvement with the child welfare system. In addition, data should be collected by age and gender, taking into consideration the characteristics of the population, analyzed by region, office and even supervisory unit level whenever possible. This level of data allows states to target their response and prioritize interventions.

Casey Family Programs supported research conducted by Chapin Hall Center for Children, which found that age is a critical factor in racial disproportionality in child welfare. They report that both placement and disparity rates are consistently higher for infants. They also found that these disparities at the county level vary in relation to characteristics of the population. Data analysis has guided Texas CPS efforts to identify problem areas and needed practice and policy changes. Data-driven planning ensures that the actions taken are relevant (both internal to DFPS/CPS and external to the community) and verifies that outcomes are indeed linked to changes in practice, policy or programming.

3) **Leadership Development** – Texas child welfare officials were committed to operationalizing a values-based leadership approach. Anti-racism initiatives and a fundamental commitment to families and communities was central to this approach. Child welfare managers and staff evaluated how their own practices and day-to-day decisions affected outcomes for children of color in care as well as their families. Part of their leadership development involved learning to lead from a position of values and character, and a commitment to shape future outcomes through immediate acts. The values underlying Texas CPS leadership activity are intended to guide leaders towards humane practices and policies in their behavior with staff, youth, families, and others.

4) **Community Engagement Model** – External stakeholders are actively engaged in the Texas approach to address racial disproportionality. This engagement model is based on the understanding that community members are best equipped to create solutions that work for their specific needs; that stakeholder buy-in is necessary for intervention success; and that their involvement is critical to sustain change over time. In Texas, there are essentially four components that define the community engagement model:

   a. *Community Awareness and Engagement*—Making the problem and issues visible, sharing the data, telling the story with the media and with constituents, enrolling community leaders, and building local allies.

   b. *Community Leadership*—Expanding the leadership beyond organizations/institutions to the level where it belongs, that is, at the community level. Participation in *Undoing Racism* training is available to reinforce the committee members as agents of social change.

c. *Community Organization*—Going to the community, being guided by it to learn what its strengths are, and hearing from residents while bringing them to the table as key informants to address their issues.
d. *Community Accountability*—Working towards desired outcomes and measurable results to achieve the ultimate goal of sustainability, and ensuring that communities own the solutions.

5) **Creating a Culturally Competent Workforce** – Developing a culturally competent workforce has included both training and skills development of current CPS personnel as well as efforts to create a diverse workforce. Trainings primarily involved the *Undoing Racism* workshop and the *Knowing Who You Are* training developed by Casey Family Programs. The state legislature appropriated funds to hire five disproportionality specialists to help move their remediation plan forward across the state.

6) **Targeted Recruitment of Foster and Adoptive Families** – Texas has increased targeted recruitment efforts for foster and adoptive parents who can meet the needs of children and youth who are waiting for permanent homes, including an expansion of the Department's faith-based effort and One Church, One Child programs. This effort has sought to decrease the number of African American children waiting for permanent homes.

Much of the work for Texas child welfare reform has been strengthened by clear and assertive leadership at both the legislative and executive branches of state government. The state legislature was very actively involved in guiding the work of this system reform effort, and developed clear accountability guidelines and requirements in Texas state law. In partnership with Casey Family Programs, Texas child welfare officials have chronicled their efforts to reduce and eliminate racial disproportionality and disparate outcomes in a publication entitled, *Engaging Communities in Taking a Stand for Children and Families,* and its accompanying Executive Summary. I would like to submit for the record a copy of this chapter as an attachment to my written testimony.

Additional Examples of Emerging and Promising State and Local Practice and Policy

Cross Systems Partnership: Child Welfare and Public School Systems – Several jurisdictions including Ramsey County, MN, Guilford County, NC, and the state of Connecticut have developed effective partnerships between their respective child welfare and public school systems. In these jurisdictions social workers have completed intensive training of school personnel on mandatory reporting responsibilities and procedures and co-located social workers in schools with the highest rates of CPS referrals. Co-location allows workers to identify children and families in need of additional supports before families enter the child welfare system. This cross system collaboration prevents unnecessary child welfare system involvement.

Private Agency Performance Based Contracting and Accountability – In Jefferson County, KY, the public child welfare agency developed and implemented a system of performance based contracting and accountability that included a data driven focus on racial disparities and cultural responsiveness in services for children and families. Private agencies and other community based organizations with public agency contracts are now required to report outcomes for children and families, including the provision of services to children and families (timeliness and effectiveness) by race and ethnicity of service providers and recipients. Organizations must demonstrate effectiveness in culturally responsive practice, an outcome data-driven determination, in order to maintain their contractual relationship with the public agency.

Identification and Engagement of Fathers, Paternal Relatives and Members of the Extended Family Support Network in Case Planning and Decision Making Process – A number of public child welfare agencies, including those in Wake County and Guilford County, NC and Des Moines, IA, realized that they had not done an effective job of identifying fathers and/or subsequently engaging them or their extended family in the discussion about their child's well-being and potential involvement in the foster care system. As a result, agencies developed formal protocols for social workers to follow in an effort to first identify fathers, and for engaging them in the case planning and subsequent decision making process regarding their children. Agencies also developed additional support programs aimed at educating fathers on how to most effectively navigate the foster care and related human service systems.

Identification of Community Based Organizations and Family Support Resources Available to Assist Families – According to the most recent federal data available, nearly one out of four children who enters foster care exits in less than six months. This suggests that many of these placements could have been prevented in the first place. However, with few home and community based resources available or known to the child welfare agencies, children and families unnecessarily endure the trauma of foster care involvement. This is particularly pervasive in communities of color. Several public child welfare agencies, including those in Connecticut, dedicated the time of one or more social workers to go into the community and identify existing resources. Connecticut child welfare staff compiled this information providing descriptions of the organizations, services offered and contact information. They then distributed this information to social services personnel, schools and other child and family serving professionals, as well as families. The community resource directories are continually updated and made available so that community members, including mandatory reporters, have information needed to refer families to the appropriate support resources when needed and appropriate.

Parent Advocate Programs – A number of jurisdictions, including Jefferson County, KY have begun to develop formal programs that match mothers and fathers, who were once involved with the foster care system, with mothers and fathers who are currently involved with the child welfare system. This approach provides support to parents attempting to navigate what is frequently a frightening, painful and very traumatic process. Research shows that when parents participate in this type of program, children experience higher rates of reunification, spend less time in foster care, experience fewer placement moves while in care, and are more likely to be placed with and/or maintain significant levels of contact with their immediate and extended family members while in care.

Deliberate and Thoughtful Engagement of Foster Youth, Alumni of Foster Care, and Birth Parents with Foster Care System Involvement in Ongoing Systems Improvement Efforts – Several public child welfare agencies, including those in Jefferson County, KY, Des Moines, IA, and Connecticut have developed effective methods of engaging youth, alumni of care, and birth parents. Their involvement has sensitized child welfare professionals to the experience of families negotiating the child protective and foster care systems, and has provided child welfare professionals with practical strategies for improving family engagement as well as youth and family compliance with case plans. Strategies include: the development of youth and birth parent boards and constituent organizations; involvement in agency training and professional development activities; testimony at agency and local government child welfare hearings; and agency reform- focused community organizing roles.

Community Outreach, Organizing and Cultural Responsiveness Strategies - Poor and sometimes hostile relationships often emerge between the predominantly Caucasian public child welfare agency workforce and the various communities of color. In Ramsey County, MN the public agency leadership developed a strategy of employing "cultural consultants" to bridge the mutual level of trust, understanding and responsiveness between the agency and the various cultural communities. The cultural consultants organized and facilitated hearings and discussion forums within the child welfare agency as well as within the community, and eventually between both. These forums and information exchange opportunities allowed for more transparency and cooperation between agency personnel and community members. Ultimately these strategies resulted in more thoughtful and sustained engagement of family members, as well as faith and civic organizations in prevention and direct family support activities. This also led to sustained opportunities for community participation in ongoing child welfare system improvement efforts.

In Woodbury County, IA, the Minority Youth and Family Initiative (MYFI) Special Native American Project Team (SNAP), created in 2004 to meet the needs of children and families in out of home care, provides active efforts to all children self-identified as American Indian. The SNAP team consists of a Supervisor, Native family liaison, Native tribal liaison and social workers. Through efforts of CINCF, team efforts have expanded to include collaborations with child protective and adoptions workers. Because SNAP team members and other local DHS staff are partners in the collaboration, SNAP efforts continue to grow and improve. Some goals of SNAP include working with relatives from the onset of placement, connecting with tribes early and often, and the involvement of the Native Liaisons from the onset of a child protective services case.

This is only a small snapshot of the exciting and promising work being done at the state and local level to address racial disproportionality in child welfare. The Alliance has created a network of state and local leaders to continue the shared learning of the BSC initiative. State leaders in more than 10 states and counties have committed to share effective strategies with one another. Per your request, we will continue to share these lessons with this Subcommittee.

Federal Policy Recommendations

1. Invest federal resources in prevention activities that keep children safely out of foster care.
2. Improve efforts to locate relatives and engage them in placement decisions that serve the best interests of the child. When family members are identified and engaged in all aspects of service delivery, the outcomes for all children are significantly improved. This is especially true for children of color.
3. Federal child welfare funds should support a range of permanency options, including reunification, adoption, and guardianship. Currently, federal funds support one form of permanency: adoption. The adoption assistance program provides financial supports to families who adopt eligible children from foster care and the adoption incentive program provides financial rewards to states that increase the number of children adopted from foster care over and above an established baseline. Support should also be available for children who exit foster care through reunification or guardianship. These modifications to funding should provide states with incentives to move children out of foster care for a full range of permanency options. In addition, federal funds should provide a full array of post-permanency services and supports to families, whenever a child exits foster care through reunification, adoption or guardianship, in order to ensure that a child remains safely in his or her permanent home. These provisions benefit all children in care. They are especially essential for children of color by strengthening the ability of extended family members and kin to provide permanent, loving homes for children when their biological parents are unable to do so.
4. Grant Indian tribes and native children and families equal access to all federal child welfare supports. In too many states, native children are placed in foster care at rates 4-5 times greater than their proportion of the population. Tribal child welfare systems are disadvantaged by the way that federal child welfare funding is provided for child welfare services. Tribes are not allowed to directly receive federal Title IV-E foster care funds, and, as a result, their ability to provide the necessary care and services for vulnerable children and their families is severely limited. Currently funds must be negotiated with the state in which the tribe is located. This pass-through approach is cumbersome, costly to tribes and inconsistently applied across states. American Indian/Alaskan Native children in the care of tribal social services agencies should receive direct

federal child welfare support by allowing Indian tribes to have direct access to Title IV-E funding.

5. Allow federal training dollars to be used to train the full continuum of workers who work with children and families who come to the attention of child welfare. Most states contract with private non-profit agencies to provide many child welfare services. In addition, many systems outside the child welfare agencies serve and impact the children and families involved in child welfare. However, current federal law limits the use of training funds to only public agency workers.
6. Collect data on the disproportionate representation of children of color in all stages of child welfare involvement at the federal level and require states to have in place a plan to collect such data at the state and regional level. In addition, mandate that states create a plan in collaboration with key stakeholders including families, birth parents, alumni of foster care, courts and other child and family serving agencies to address any disparities that are revealed.

We applaud this Subcommittee and the House for passing H.R. 6307, which includes provisions that address a number of these recommendations.

In closing, as I participate here today I do so with the strong belief that change is possible and that the outcomes that we seek can be achieved – but time is of the essence. On average, each day in America, approximately 800 children are removed from their homes and placed in foster care, approximately half of those children were children of color. I thank you for seeking real change on their behalf, for having the courage to address the issue of racial disproportionality in child welfare and for seeking to learn about what is working at the state and local level. I also thank you again Mr. Chairman, Congressman Weller, and Subcommittee members for the opportunity to share Casey Family Programs' perspective with you today. Casey Family Programs is available as a resource to the Subcommittee, or to individual members, for more specific data, best practices or technical assistance as you continue to pursue policy solutions to this issue.

Thank you.

In: Foster Care and African-American Youth
Editor: Joanna Kaczmarek
ISBN: 978-1-60741-541-1

Chapter 7

TRENDS IN FOSTER CARE AND ADOPTION—FY 2002-FY 2007

Joanna Kaczmarek

DISCUSSION OF "TRENDS" CHART

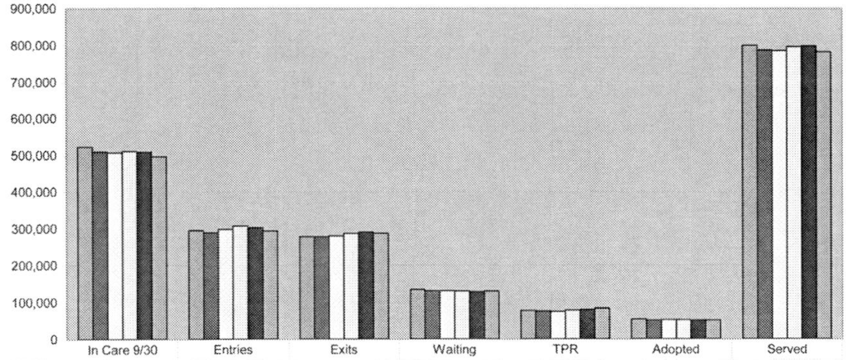

	In Care 9/30	Entries	Exits	Waiting	TPR	Adopted	Served
FY 2002	523,000	295,000	278,000	134,000	77,000	53,000	800,000
FY 2003	510,000	289,000	278,000	131,000	76,000	51,000	787,000
FY 2004	507,000	298,000	280,000	131,000	74,000	52,000	786,000
FY 2005	511,000	307,000	287,000	130,000	78,000	52,000	797,000
FY 2006	509,000	303,000	290,000	129,000	80,000	51,000	799,000
FY 2007	496,000	293,000	287,000	130,000	84,000	51,000	783,000

Source: AFCARS data, U.S. Children's Bureau, Adminstration for Children, Youth and Families

The data in the chart were submitted to the Adoption and Foster Care Analysis and Reporting System (AFCARS) by States, the District of Columbia and Puerto Rico by September 1, 2008.

Sub-population Definitions

1. **In foster care on the last day of the federal fiscal year (September 30):** This is an estimated count of all the children in foster care on the last day of the year. An individual child is included in the count for each year for which he or she is in foster care on the last day.

2. **Entering care during the federal fiscal year:** This is an estimated count of all children who enter foster care **during** the year. An individual child is counted only once for each year, even if the child entered, exited and reentered care during the year. If an individual child entered in one year and then exits and re-enters in a subsequent year, he or she is included in the count of entries for both years.

3. **Exiting care during the federal fiscal year:** This is an estimated count of all children who exited foster care during the fiscal year **at the end of their most recent foster care episode**. An individual child is counted only once for each year, even if the child exited, re-entered and exited again during the year. If an individual child exits care in one year and then re-enters and exits again in a subsequent year, he or she is included in the count of exits for both years.

4. **Whose parental rights have been terminated (TPR):** This is an estimated count of the children in care o**n the last day** of the year who are both waiting for adoption and whose parental rights have been terminated. An individual child is counted only once for each year. An individual child is included in the count for each year that he or she has these characteristics on the last day of the year.

5. **Waiting to be adopted:** This is an estimated count of all children who are waiting to be adopted **on the last day** of the year. An individual child is included in the count for each year in which he or she is waiting to be adopted on the last day. There is no federal definition for children waiting

to be adopted. For the purposes of this analysis, children waiting to be adopted include children with a goal of adoption and/or whose parental rights have been terminated. Children whose parental rights have been terminated, who are 16 years old and older, and who have a goal of emancipation are excluded from the "waiting" population. An individual child is included in the count for each year that he or she has these characteristics on the last day of the year.

6. **Adopted:** This is an estimated count of all children adopted **during the year** with public child welfare agency involvement. An individual child is counted only once for each year. In rare cases when a child is adopted multiple times, the child will be counted in each year he or she is adopted.

7. **Served:** This is an estimated count of all children who were in the public foster care system **during the year**. This number is the sum of two mutually exclusive groups of children: the children who are already in care on the first day of the fiscal year (as of October 1) and the children who enter foster care during the year. An individual child is counted only once for each year.

TECHNICAL DISCUSSION

Ideally, the count in # 1 (in foster care on the last day of the year) plus the count in # 3 (exiting foster care during the fiscal year) should equal the count in # 7 (served). They are equal in FY 2006 and FY 2007, but they are not equal in FY 2002- FY 2005. The difference in those years is 1,000, or less than one tenth of one percent. Most of the difference can be attributed to estimation procedures and rounding.

Examination of the relationship between the number of exits and entries for each year gives the erroneous impression that the number of entries each year is greater than the number of exits even though the number of children in care on September 30 may be steady, be declining, or even be increasing but at a much slower pace than the exit numbers imply. This occurs because in the AFCARS database each child is counted only once and the information included on the child in the database is from their most recent foster care episode. However, there are some children who were in foster care on the first day of the year and exited and re-entered during the year one or more times prior to entering their most recent foster care episode. In addition, they remained in foster care through the last day of the fiscal year (September 30) in their most recent foster care episode. In these circumstances, the exit associated with their "in care" status on the first day of the year is not counted. We estimate that the number of these uncounted exits exceeds 10,000 annually.

There is also a data quality issue which has an impact on the number of exits. AFCARS data are submitted every six months covering a six month period. Sometimes a child who is reported during one six month period does not appear in the next period, and there is no record that the child exited. Reviews of these cases have shown that almost all of these are situations in which the child actually exited, but the exit was not reported to AFCARS. However, because the actual number of these "dropped" exits cannot be calculated, they have not been accounted for in the exit count. As this situation has been pointed out to states, the data quality has improved and the number of dropped exits has decreased. The number per year in FY 2002-FY 2006 is estimated to range between 8,000 and 10,000.

Data Discussion

The data show that the decline in the estimated number of children in foster care on the last day of each federal fiscal year (September 30) resumed in FY 2007 after pausing in FY 2005 and FY 2006. Between FY 2004 and FY 2005 the estimated number of children in care on the last day of the fiscal year increased from 507,000 in FY 2004 to 511,000 in FY 2005 and dropped slightly to 509,000 in FY 2006. For the first time since AFCARS data have been reported, in FY 2007 the estimated number of children in care on September 30 dropped below 500,000 to 496,000. A similar pattern is seen in the total estimated number of children served during these years. After declining since FY 1998, the estimated number of children served increased from 786,000 in FY 2004 to 797,000 in FY 2005 and 799,000 in FY 2006. The total number of children served in FY 2007 is estimated to be 783,000, the lowest number since AFCARS data have been reported.

After remaining under 300,000 until FY 2004, the estimated number of entries into foster care exceeded 300,000 in both FY 2005 and FY 2006 at 307,000 and 303,000, respectively. In FY 2007, the estimated number entries into foster care dropped to 293,000. The estimated number of exits which had increased between FY 2004 and FY 2006 from 280,000 to 290,000, declined slightly to 287,000 in FY 2007, excluding the exits identified in the second and third paragraphs of the technical discussion.

Since FY 2003, the estimated number of waiting children has been approximately 130,000 on the last day of each year. The estimated number of waiting children whose parental rights had been terminated as of the last day of the year has been increasing from 74,000 in FY 2004, to 78,000 in FY 2005, and to 80,000 in FY 2005. The estimated number reached 84,000 in FY 2007, the highest number since AFCARS data have been reported.

INDEX

A

AAP, 25
abstinence, 83
accountability, x, 19, 70, 77, 79, 80, 81, 98, 102, 126, 127
accuracy, 46
adequate housing, 10, 107
administration, 46, 50, 65
administrative, 8, 21, 27, 36, 50, 64, 71
administrators, 4, 12, 15, 104, 114
adolescents, 50, 83, 84
adoption incentives, 113
adult, 78, 89, 95, 110, 118, 122
adulthood, 104, 111
adults, 71, 89, 104
advocacy, 115
agents, 126
aging, 111, 112
aid, 5, 15
allies, 125
alternative, 3, 14, 16, 17, 50, 104
alternatives, 51
amendments, 83
antipsychotic, 50
appendix, 20, 27, 30, 61, 62
application, 51
attachment, 126
auditing, 4, 80
authority, 19, 51, 112
availability, 5, 25, 78, 81, 82, 89, 90, 110, 112, 114
avoidance, 97
awareness, 82, 91, 96

B

barrier, 107, 110
barriers, 16, 78, 90, 91, 95, 108, 110, 119
basic needs, 113
behavior, 19, 29, 125
behavioral problems, 39, 111
benefits, 37, 44, 51, 88, 90, 103, 104
bias, 2, 5, 9, 10, 12, 13, 123
biological parents, 48, 130
bipartisan, 113
bipolar, 74
bipolar disorder, 74
birth, 128, 131
block grants, 8, 16, 20, 21
bonds, 89
bonus, 74
brothers, 118, 119

C

caps, 16
care model, 36
caregiver, 54

caregivers, 14, 31, 51, 52, 124
certifications, 84
check-ups, 40
child abuse, 3, 19, 122
child maltreatment, 108
child protection, 8
child protective services, 11, 124, 129
classes, 89, 107
clinical diagnosis, 74
clinics, 42, 43, 47, 60
collaboration, 14, 30, 55, 61, 122, 127, 129, 131
communities, 10, 38, 91, 106, 113, 114, 122, 123, 124, 125, 126, 128, 129
Community Based Organizations, 128
community support, 2
community-based services, 47
competency, 2, 5, 13
compliance, 27, 113, 116, 128
components, 122, 125
conformity, 72
Congressional Budget Office, 25, 74
consensus, 15
consent, 50, 55, 57
construction, 55
consultants, 58, 59, 72, 129
consulting, 123
contingency, 72
continuity, 31, 33, 44
contractors, 80, 104
contracts, 57, 118, 127
control, 30, 74, 84, 97
control group, 84
costs, 8, 21, 32, 37, 71, 74, 88
counseling, 10, 71, 87, 107
courts, 4, 112, 131
covering, 44, 92, 136
CPS, 107, 122, 125, 126, 127
credentialing, 33
credit, 78, 90
credit history, 78, 90
crisis intervention, 47
CRS, 107, 108, 115
cultural heritage, 119
culture, 114, 115, 118, 119
curriculum, 97

D

daily living, 87, 88, 90, 104
danger, 51
data analysis, 15
data collection, 13, 15, 103
database, 48, 55, 56, 82, 135
death, 19
decision makers, 2, 5, 9, 10, 13
decision making, 12, 13, 113, 114, 127
decisions, 4, 13, 19, 21, 36, 54, 71, 102, 112, 125, 130
deficiency, 25, 37
definition, 134
delinquent behavior, 19
delivery, x, 23, 24, 27, 28, 36, 45, 57, 60, 63, 75, 80, 91, 130
dentists, 34
Department of Health and Human Services, x, 4, 20, 25, 26, 61, 63, 66, 69, 74, 77, 80, 110, 115
depression, 30
developmental disabilities, 47
disability, 11, 19, 20
disabled, 83
discretionary, 59
dissatisfaction, 89, 90
distribution, 40, 64
diversity, 14
doctors, 4, 29, 55
dosage, 51
draft, 6, 17, 30, 61, 75
drug interaction, 51
drugs, 29, 50, 57, 109
duplication, 46, 52

E

education, 18, 62, 83, 87, 91, 97, 101, 103
elderly, 8
electronic systems, 52
eligibility criteria, 8, 32, 33, 36, 71

emancipation, 89, 115, 116, 135
emotional disorder, 59
emotional health, 44
employment, 78, 79, 90, 94, 95, 97, 104, 122
employment status, 94
engagement, 28, 64, 90, 111, 124, 125, 128, 129
enrollment, 73
epilepsy, 74
equity, 123
ethnic groups, 108, 110, 114
ethnicity, 3, 11, 107, 108, 124, 127
examinations, 24, 28, 46, 57, 73
expenditures, 36, 72
expertise, 58, 59
exposure, 97, 109

F

faith, x, 14, 105, 126, 129
familial, 12, 111
family environment, 110
family members, 13, 108, 128, 129, 130
family support, 16, 71, 129
federal funds, ix, x, 3, 6, 8, 16, 18, 21, 32, 36, 71, 72, 77, 82, 103, 113, 130
federal government, 8, 19, 36, 70, 96, 102
federal law, 8, 14, 19, 20, 27, 36, 38, 71, 118, 131
fee, 36, 46, 47, 72, 104
feeding, 32
fees, 88
females, 10
financial support, 12, 14, 88, 130
financing, 36, 60, 71
flexibility, 26, 32, 58, 83
focusing, 29, 33
Food and Drug Administration, 57
forgiveness, 114
fragility, 109
freedom, 16

G

gender, 124
goals, 4, 17, 34, 48, 49, 72, 79, 81, 84, 91, 93, 122, 129
government, vi, 4, 8, 19, 36, 70, 80, 96, 102, 106, 113, 126, 129
grants, 8, 16, 20, 21, 37, 56
groups, 15, 40, 60, 64, 80, 84, 91, 95, 108, 110, 111, 114, 135
guardian, 8
guidance, 19, 27, 41, 48, 93, 95, 116
guidelines, ix, 39, 126

H

harm, 10
Health and Human Services, x, 4, 20, 24, 25, 26, 61, 62, 63, 66, 69, 74, 77, 80, 110, 115
health care professionals, 44
health education, 36, 94
health information, 32, 52, 55, 56, 74
health insurance, 72, 87
health problems, 59
health services, x, 23, 27, 28, 31, 34, 36, 46, 55, 63, 79, 81, 89, 104, 107
health status, 31
healthcare, 37
hearing, 36, 126
high school, 83, 118
homelessness, 79, 111
hospital, 42, 43, 46
hospitalization, 47
hospitals, 42, 43
households, 10, 108
housing, 2, 10, 11, 32, 78, 81, 83, 87, 88, 90, 91, 94, 95, 96, 97, 103, 104, 107
human, 37, 127
human immunodeficiency virus, 37
humane, 125

I

identification, 24, 28, 38, 41, 44, 48, 61

identity, 106
images, 31, 53
immunization, 25, 29, 45, 49, 52, 54, 55, 57
immunodeficiency, 25
implementation, 5, 26, 49, 60, 79, 82, 84, 111, 112, 116
incarceration, 30, 111
incentives, 45, 46, 90, 130
incidence, 19
inclusion, 41
income, 10, 11, 14, 20, 50, 71, 108
independence, 60, 78, 81, 88, 90, 95
indicators, 33, 44, 64
inequity, 124
infants, 15, 108, 109, 125
information exchange, 56, 129
information sharing, 91
information systems, 33, 71
Information Technology, 74
infrastructure, 85
innovation, 91
instability, 111
institutions, 47, 126
instructor quality, 89
instruments, 41
integration, 60
integrity, 19, 71, 102
interactions, 51
interest groups, 64
intervention, 39, 47, 60, 61, 112, 125
interview, 42, 50, 64
interviews, ix, 1, 4, 11, 27, 63, 64, 94
investment, 104

J

judge, 4, 50
judges, 10
jurisdiction, 64
jurisdictions, 122, 123, 124, 127, 128
justice, 106

L

laws, 14, 19, 27
leadership, 113, 118, 124, 125, 126, 129
learning, 125, 129
legislation, 4, 6, 17, 110, 113, 114, 119
licensing, 33
likelihood, 28, 49
limitations, 28, 64, 93
links, 38, 60, 75
local government, 106, 129
long period, 111
losses, 119
low-income, 10, 11, 14, 50, 71

M

magnetic, vi
maintenance, 8, 21, 48
maltreatment, 108, 114, 115
management, 29, 37, 48, 49, 53, 57, 72, 74, 75
management practices, 29
married couples, 10
maternal, 37, 65, 72
measurement, 103
measures, 6, 17, 25, 54, 56, 98, 111
media, 125
median, 108
medical care, 32, 47, 49, 55, 57, 74
medical expertise, 25, 48
medical services, 29, 48, 49
medication, 50, 51
medications, 24, 28, 29, 32, 33, 45, 50, 51, 53, 55, 57, 60, 71, 74, 103
membership, 20, 109
men, 89
mental illness, 44
mentoring, 89, 97, 104
mentoring program, 89
metropolitan area, 27
minorities, 110, 112
minority, 6, 11, 14, 20, 110, 114
misunderstanding, 5, 9, 10, 13
models, 89

mood, 29, 74
mood swings, 74
moratorium, 37
morning, 121
mothers, 128
multidisciplinary, 47

N

nation, x, 10, 26, 71, 83, 105, 109, 111, 119, 121, 122
national origin, 21
neglect, 3, 10, 13, 19, 26, 39, 106, 107, 119, 122
negotiating, 128
non-profit, 131
normal, 43
nurses, 29, 45, 48, 49, 55
nursing, 74

O

Offices of Congressional Relations and Public Affairs, 62
oral, 47
orthodontists, 47
oversight, 4, 19, 26, 33, 34, 44, 50, 51, 71, 93, 98, 102, 113

P

parenthood, 111
parenting, 10, 107
partnership, 126
partnerships, 60, 61, 123, 127
paternal, 5, 14
patients, 32, 56, 57, 74
pediatric, 40, 46
pediatrician, 44
per capita, 72
perception, 10
periodic, 19, 88
periodicity, 40
permit, 24
personnel costs, 74
physical health, 17, 33, 38, 41, 44, 104
physicians, 24, 28, 33, 34, 42, 43, 46
plague, 122
planning, 13, 39, 48, 88, 103, 109, 125, 127
police, 4, 10
policymakers, 15
poor, 10, 11, 111, 124
postsecondary education, 83, 87
poverty, ix, 2, 5, 9, 10, 106, 108, 114, 124
poverty rate, 108
prevention, x, 94, 105, 107, 114, 124, 129, 130
preventive, 3, 16, 28, 34, 40, 43, 44, 55
primary care, 42, 48, 60, 72
privacy, 52, 55
private, x, 5, 58, 60, 72, 91, 95, 105, 114, 131
private sector, 95
professional development, 129
profit, 131
program outcomes, 79
programming, 125
progress reports, 82, 92, 93, 95, 98
protection, 8, 52, 112
protective factors, 114
protocol, 98, 127
psychiatrist, 51
psychiatrists, 47
psychotropic drug, 50
psychotropic drugs, 50
psychotropic medications, 25, 29, 45, 50, 51, 55, 57, 60, 74
public funding, 47
public funds, 19, 71, 102
public health, 42, 48, 55, 58

Q

quality assurance, 25, 29, 52, 56
quality improvement, 43
quality of service, 57

R

race, ix, 3, 11, 16, 19, 21, 107, 108, 110, 115, 124, 127
racial equity, 123
racial minorities, 108, 111
racism, 114, 124, 125
random, 84, 104
random assignment, 84, 104
range, x, 13, 33, 37, 58, 59, 72, 85, 88, 91, 103, 105, 109, 130, 136
reading, 97
reality, 113
recall, 49, 74
recognized tribe, 118
recruiting, 2, 5, 6, 11, 14, 17, 21, 89
registries, 52
regular, 24, 28, 75
regulation, 32, 36
regulations, 19, 34, 36, 72, 79, 82
regulatory requirements, 27
reimbursement, 32, 46, 72
relationship, 97, 104, 114, 123, 127, 135
relationships, 89, 91, 129
relatives, ix, 2, 5, 6, 7, 12, 14, 18, 74, 110, 129, 130
reliability, 19, 71, 102
remediation, 126
reporters, 10, 107, 128
research design, 37, 95
reservation, 8, 71, 114
residential, x, 7, 105
resources, 16, 17, 46, 78, 81, 82, 90, 91, 96, 111, 112, 114, 124, 128, 130
responsiveness, 127, 129
restructuring, 2, 6, 17
returns, 74
reunification, 8, 9, 71, 107, 108, 111, 128, 130
rewards, 130
Rhode Island, 20, 86, 100, 102, 103
risk, 10, 13, 16, 38, 40, 59, 94, 97, 108, 111, 122, 123
rural, 46, 78, 81, 89, 90
rural areas, 46, 78, 81, 89, 90

S

safety, 25, 29, 32, 33, 37, 48, 50, 71, 124
sample, 19, 39, 44, 60, 71, 94, 104
sampling, 94
savings, 122
school, 44, 83, 88, 107, 111, 117, 127, 128
school performance, 111
search, 2, 92, 95, 104
searches, 14
searching, 5
security, 52, 55
seizures, 74
selecting, 63
service provider, 14, 36, 89, 90, 91, 96, 127
sexual abuse, 109
shape, 10, 119, 125
sharing, 29, 52, 54, 55, 60, 74, 91, 125
short supply, 31, 107
shortage, 17
sibling, 20, 109
siblings, 117, 118
side effects, 51
sign, 39, 111
similarity, 19
sites, 15, 60, 88, 123
skills, 10, 87, 88, 90, 97, 104, 126
social change, 126
social services, 8, 82, 96, 128, 130
social systems, 95
social workers, 44, 114, 127, 128, 129
spectrum, 106
stability, 17, 97, 115
stages, 15, 39, 111, 115, 131
stakeholder, 125
stakeholders, 27, 41, 58, 125, 131
standards, 4, 24, 28, 32, 33, 36, 40, 55, 57, 71, 73, 80, 84, 95, 112
statistics, 106
statutory, 27
strength, 72
stress, 107
subgroups, 45, 46
subsidies, 2, 6, 8, 16, 17, 20, 21, 90
subsidy, 2, 88

substance use, 75
summer, 118
supervision, 26, 33
supply, 88
support services, 2, 5, 9, 10, 12, 16, 60, 71, 114
surgeons, 47
sustainability, 126
sweat, 118
syndrome, 25, 37

T

tangible, 103
tangible benefits, 103
teachers, 4, 10
team members, 129
territory, 87
testimony, ix, x, 1, 4, 19, 77, 78, 79, 80, 82, 95, 126, 129
threat, 30
time frame, 41, 111
timing, 24, 28, 36, 38
title, 32, 33, 36, 71, 72
tracking, 15, 79, 82
tradition, 119
transition, 82, 83, 84, 89, 90, 95, 111
transition to adulthood, 83
transmission, 55
transparency, 129
transportation, 47, 88
trauma, 128
travel, 47
trial, 72
tribes, 112, 113, 118, 119, 122, 129, 130
truancy, 19
trust, 14, 129
turnover, 91
tutoring, 97, 103

U

unemployment, 111
uniform, 78, 82, 92, 95, 98, 104
universities, 51, 58
updating, 29, 40, 52
urban areas, 43, 78, 81, 90

V

values, 19, 71, 102, 125
variables, 54
variation, 98
victims, 107, 122
violence, 30
virus, 25, 37
visible, 125
vision, x, 36, 54, 105, 122
vocational, 104
vocational training, 104
voicing, 119
vouchers, 83

W

wages, 111
websites, 75
welfare law, 19
welfare reform, 124, 126
wellbeing, 25, 29, 49, 61, 111, 116, 127
workers, 44, 49, 55, 84, 110, 127, 129, 131
workforce, 83, 91, 104, 114, 126, 129

Y

young adults, 104
younger children, 11
youth transition, 78, 81, 82, 90